THE ESSENTIAL
GUIDE TO
CONTEMPORARY
LITERATURE

Roddy Doyle

SERIES EDITORS
Jonathan Noakes
and
Margaret Reynolds
with Vanessa Berman

Also available in Vintage Living Texts

American Fiction

Martin Amis

Margaret Atwood

Louis de Bernières

A. S. Byatt

Sebastian Faulks

John Fowles

Susan Hill

Ian McEwan

Toni Morrison

Iris Murdoch

Salman Rushdie

Jeanette Winterson

'I didn't realise just how good the series was until I started working closely with it. The questions are so thoughtful and probing, and the analysis provided allows the students to lift their own understanding. The texts really do occupy their own niche between guides purely for teachers and the ubiquitous student crib, and are much better than either.'
Michael Parker, Head of English, Newington College, NSW, Australia

'This is a terrific series. The text and the reader's response are at the heart of these guides; the tone is authoritative but never dogmatic, while the style is enthusiastic and approachable. The series is aptly named – not only are the subjects still alive, so too are the guides.'
Lucy Webster, *The English Magazine*

'*Vintage Living Texts* are very modern. They are certainly democratic as they give the literary text to the reader, prompting personal critical response without suggesting what those responses should be. They will be a blessing to teachers and students.'
Iain Finlayson, *The Times* Play Magazine

'These guides, designed to reflect the National Curriculum, are likely to appeal also to university students, and those who take their reading group seriously.'
Independent Magazine

'In addition to sixth formers and undergraduates, the series also works well for those taking the International Baccalaureate or on EFL courses.'
Liz Thomson, *Publishing News*

VINTAGE
LIVING
TEXTS

Roddy Doyle

THE ESSENTIAL GUIDE
TO CONTEMPORARY
LITERATURE

The Barrytown Trilogy:
The Commitments
The Snapper
The Van

Paddy Clarke Ha Ha Ha
The Woman Who Walked Into Doors

VINTAGE

Published by Vintage 2004

2 4 6 8 10 9 7 5 3 1

First published in Great Britain in 2004 by Vintage
Random House, 20 Vauxhall Bridge Road,
London SWIV 2SA

Random House Australia (Pty) Limited
20 Alfred Street, Milsons Point, Sydney,
New South Wales 2061, Australia

Random House New Zealand Limited
18 Poland Road, Glenfield,
Auckland 10, New Zealand

Random House (Pty) Limited
Endulini, 5A Jubilee Road, Parktown 2193, South Africa

The Random House Group Limited Reg. No. 954009
www.randomhouse.co.uk

A CIP catalogue record for this book is available from the British Library

ISBN 0 099 452197

Papers used by Random House are natural, recyclable products made
from wood grown in sustainable forests; the manufacturing processes
conform to the environmental regulations of the country of origin.

Typeset by Palimpsest Book Production Limited, Polmont, Stirlingshire

Printed and bound in Great Britain by
Bookmarque Ltd, Croydon, Surrey

CONTENTS

Paddy Clarke Ha Ha Ha

The Woman Who Walked Into Doors

VINTAGE LIVING TEXTS: REFERENCE

Acknowledgements

We owe grateful thanks to all at Random House. Most of all our debt is to Rachel Cugnoni and her team at Vintage – especially to Ali Reynolds – Jason Arthur, Liz Foley, Katherine Fry and Jack Murphy who have given us generous and unfailing support. Thanks also to Caroline Michel, Marcella Edwards, Philippa Brewster and Georgina Capel, Michael Meredith, Angela Leighton, Harriet Marland, to all our colleagues and friends, and to our partners and families. We would also like to thank the teachers and students at schools and colleges around the country who have taken part in our trialling process, and who have responded so readily and warmly to our requests for advice. And finally, our grateful thanks to Roddy Doyle who alone knows how kind he has been twice over.

VINTAGE LIVING TEXTS

Preface

About this series

Vintage Living Texts: The Essential Guide to Contemporary Literature is a new concept in reading guides. Our aim is to provide readers of all kinds with an intelligent and accessible introduction to key works of contemporary literature. Each guide suggests techniques for reading important contemporary novels, and offers a variety of back-up materials that will give you ways into the text – without ever telling you what to think.

Content

All the books reproduce an extensive interview with the author, conducted exclusively for this series. This is not to say that we believe that the author's word is law. Of course it isn't. Once his or her book has gone out into the world he or she becomes simply yet another – if singularly competent – reader. This series recognises that an author's contribution may be valuable, and intriguing, but it puts the reader in control.

Every title in the series is author-focused and covers at

least three of their novels, along with relevant biographical, bibliographical, contextual and comparative material.

How to use this series

In the reading activities that make up the core of each book you will see that you are asked to do two things. One comes from the text; that is, we suggest what you should focus on, whether it's a theme, the language or the narrative method. The other concentrates on your own response. We want you to think about how you are reading and what skills you are bringing to bear in doing that reading. So this part is very much about you, the reader.

The point is that there are many ways of responding to a text. You could concentrate on the methods you might use to compare this text with others. In that case, look for the sections headed 'Compare'. Or you might want to do something more individual, and analyse how you are reacting to a text and what it means to you, in which case, pick out the approaches labelled 'Imagine' or 'Ask Yourself'.

Of course, it may well be that you are reading these texts for an examination. In that case you will have to go for the more traditional methods of literary criticism and look for the responses that tell you to 'Discuss' or 'Analyse'. Whichever level you (or your students) are at, you will find that there is something here for everyone. However, we're not suggesting that you stick solely to the approaches we offer, or that you tackle all of the exercises laid out here. Choose whatever most interests you, or whatever best suits your purposes.

Who are these books for?

Students will find that these guides are like a good teacher. They introduce the life and work of the author, set each novel in its context, explain key ideas and literary critical terms as they arise, suggest comparative exercises in a number of media, and ask focused questions to encourage a well-informed, analytical approach to reading the novels in a way that is rigorous, but still entertaining.

Teachers will find in this series a rich source of ideas for teaching contemporary novels and their contexts, particularly at AS, A and undergraduate levels. The exercises on each text have been tailored to meet the various assessment objectives laid down in the subject criteria for GCE AS and GCE A Level and the International Baccalaureate in English Literature, and are explained in such a way that they can easily be selected and fitted into a lesson plan. Given the diversity of ways in which the awarding bodies have devised their specifications to meet these assessment objectives, a wide range of exercises is offered. We've had fun devising the plans, and we hope they'll be fun for you when you come to teach and learn with them.

And if you are neither a teacher nor a student of contemporary literature, but someone reading for your own pleasure? Well, if you've ever wanted someone to introduce you to a novelist's work in a way that will let you trust your own judgement and read more confidently, then this guide is also for you.

Whoever you are, we hope that you will enjoy using these books and that they will send you back to the novels to find new pleasures.

All page references to *The Commitments, The Snapper, The Van, Paddy Clarke Ha Ha Ha* and *The Woman Who Walked Into Doors* in this text refer to the Vintage editions.

Roddy Doyle

Introduction

Roddy Doyle appeared on the literary scene in 1979 with an irreverent story about how the miraculous vision of the Virgin Mary, which had appeared a hundred years earlier at the holy shrine of Knock in the west of Ireland, was also the mother of the nationalist hero Patrick Pearse (her impossibly premature delivery hastened on by the bad state of the roads at the time). A rumour circulated that Doyle was then engaged on a novel whose title was to be *Your Granny was a Hunger Striker*. According to Colm Tóibín, although Doyle was planning his novel at the height of a wave of sympathy for IRA martyrs, hunger striking while imprisoned in Northern Ireland, this work was to be a *comic* novel. But, says Tóibín, 'although brought up in the bosom of the Fianna Fáil party and the Catholic Church . . . [I too] wished only for jokes on these matters'.

The planned novel turned out to be a chimera. It never did materialise, and Doyle's first novel was *The Commitments*, published in 1987. But, if only for its title, this early sighted volume still makes an appropriate appearance in the history of Doyle's work. The mix of the homely and the highly politicised, the blend of everyday language and the extremes of experience is typical of Doyle's scope and vision. It is also appropriate that his rumoured novel turned out to be a phantom, because Doyle's work is full of the ghosts and shadows of people and things that are real even though they don't exist.

At the beginning of his 1999 novel *A Star Called Henry*, the narrator, Henry Smart, is reminded by his teenage mother, hopelessly aged by poverty, starvation, alcohol and childbearing, that he is not the first to own that name. Her first-born, long dead in infancy, was the true Henry who goes on living in her imagination as a star – she points out a particular star in the sky while huddled night after night on the steps of a fetid Dublin basement. The living character of Henry will be haunted by that star – as he is also haunted by the ghost of his father who disappears, leaving only his mahogany false leg which later becomes young Henry's trademark, touchstone and killer weapon.

None of Doyle's characters appear without some sense of history – often someone else's history – surrounding them. There is a connectedness and a linking, an integration that makes his apparently closed worlds broader, more integrated and more widely sympathetic. It is interesting that Doyle has recently used the same motif of the remembered family in writing the story of his own parents and their past in *Rory and Ita* (2002). But this is a matter of literary method, not a personal obsession.

Doyle's use of interlinked characters and interconnecting themes, throughout his work, begins with *The Commitments*. In a tiny scene that is easy to miss, Jimmy Rabbitte is interviewing his workmate Declan as the potential lead singer for the new band. He takes him up to his room to talk about it. On the stairs they pass Sharon, Jimmy's sister. Declan is interested. Sharon tells him to 'go an' shite'.

And that's it. Sharon disappears, the novel gets on with the story of the band. But some years later Doyle takes us back to

Sharon when she finds herself unluckily pregnant after the father of one of her own teenage friends leaps on her in a car park because she's drunk and feeling too sick to do anything about it. *The Snapper* is Sharon's story. In another example, Bimbo, one of Jimmy Sr's drinking mates in *The Snapper*, reappears as a major character and the purchaser of the eponymous chipper in *The Van*.

But the best-known example of Doyle filling in the 'back story', or the parallel story, of one of his own characters relates to Paula Spencer who is *The Woman Who Walked Into Doors*. She first appeared in Doyle's imagination as a character in a television series called *The Family* which was broadcast in 1994. As Doyle said at the time: 'I was well into the novel when *The Family* came out and I already knew that Paula's episode in that series, though the best thing I had ever written, was not enough: that there was her past to be looked at and probably her future. I had to give Paula a chance to explain why: why she married this man in the first place, and why she stayed with him.'

It's a telling remark. Doyle 'had to give Paula a chance to explain'. Which means that she lived, as far as he was concerned – she had to have a voice and he had to listen. It's the same with all his characters, and it's one reason why they all have parallel existences just on the other side of his pages where they keep coming and going in his imagination. Sharon walks down the stairs in *The Commitments* and into *The Snapper*; Bimbo leaves the Hikers in *The Snapper* and sets up a new life in *The Van*. There is even a short story by Doyle called 'Vincent' about one of the bartenders in the Hikers who serves 'Mr Rabbitte' and his pals.

Doyle's inclusive imagination extends into history – both the distant past and the recent past – in much the same way. In *A Star Called Henry*, his tricks come across as delicious jokes – as if we are always just on the margin of events and if only we could just see a little over the shoulders of that crowd, or through that window, we would truly see history in the making. So Henry tells us that it was he – not, as the history books say, William Oman – who played 'The Last Post' at the grave of O'Donovan Rossa. So Henry tells us that he asked to sign the Irish Proclamation of Independence but was told that – at fourteen – he was too young. And that, so he tells us, is why his name comes to be absent.

But if these seem like games in *A Star Called Henry*, the same techniques tell a profound truth in *The Barrytown Trilogy*, in *The Woman Who Walked Into Doors* and in *Rory and Ita*. For the fact is that history is around us all the time, and it's not always the major events that contribute to the history that helps make us what we are. In *The Woman Who Walked Into Doors*, Paula realises that she cannot remember any songs from the 1980s though the radio was on all the time. Why? 'What did I do in the 80s? I walked into doors. I got up off the floor. I became an alcoholic. I discovered that I was poor, that I'd no right to the hope I'd started out with' (p. 204). Popular history, says Doyle's fiction, is real history too. It may even be that it's more real than official history.

Doyle is interested in popular history, popular songs and popular culture – all grand terms – for the very simple reason that he is interested in people. His imaginary people live vividly in his imaginary world, but above all, his imaginary people speak to him. From the first instance it is the voices of his characters that make them come alive. In the interview included here, he speaks about how he came to find a voice as a novelist because he listened to the voices of his characters.

From the publication of *The Commitments* on, reviewers and critics have tried to pin down this distinctive method. Too often they think of it as a trick, or a technique, when it is, in fact, the very essence of his work and not an artificial overlay. As a result his novels have been described as 'dialogue novels', or 'ventriloquist novels', or even 'karaoke novels' because of their insistent soundtracks. But those fragmented soundtracks represent the richness of the conscious life quite as much as any laboured philosophising. We are what we hear, what we see, what we feel, what we touch, quite as much as what we remember and what we think.

We are also what we read. If you look closely, you will see that reading goes on in all of Doyle's novels. It's not always obvious. Sometimes it seems to appear only as a sly joke – like Darren in *The Van* trying to write an essay on the proposition that 'complexity of thought and novelty in the use of language sometimes create an apparent obscurity in the poetry of Gerard Manley Hopkins' while his family 'eff and blind' around him. You need to know quite a lot about Hopkins – his Anglo-Irish background, his priesthood, his painful struggles with his conscience, and, above all, his innovation with rhythm and language – to get the full force of the reference. Or else – you need to know none of it at all. Doyle never forces anything on his readers.

If you are attuned to these references, you'll find them throughout Doyle's fiction – Veronica reading Golding's *Lord of the Flies* in *The Van* while Jimmy Sr struggles with Dumas's *The Man in the Iron Mask*, only to find that he gets on better with Dickens's *David Copperfield*. There are many reasons why Doyle employs these cross-references but he leaves it up to the reader to think about why.

If you do choose to think about it, you will be rewarded. In *The Commitments* the band turns the Motown hit 'Night Train' into 'Dublin soul' by reinventing all the cities of Southern America as sites on the suburban map of Dublin: 'STARTIN' OFF IN CONNOLLY . . . MOVIN' ON OU' TO KILLESTER . . . HARMONSTOWN RAHENY . . . AN' DON'T FORGET KILBARRACK – THE HOME O' THE BLUES' (p. 92). These are parallel worlds, in the song and the scene, in the lives of the band and their audience, in the lives of these novels, and in our lives, as the readers of these novels.

In *A Star Called Henry* Doyle plays a similar game – except, as ever, it's not a game, but a truth. At the moment when Henry Smart is being born, his Granny Nash, already old and decrepit, is beginning to learn to read by picking out the words in the newsprint set to cover the floor ready for the blood and the afterbirth. Years on, even more impossibly old and decrepit, Granny Nash is an expert reader, but she demands that Henry bring her books only by women and her favourites bear titles like *Behind the Scenes: or, Thirty Years a Slave and Four Years in the White House,* or *The Wonderful Adventures of Mrs Seacole in Many Lands,* or *The History of Mary Prince, a West Indian Slave, Related by Herself.* She also reads Mary Wollstonecraft's *Vindication of the Rights of Woman,* but she isn't interested in Harriet Beecher Stowe's *Uncle Tom's Cabin* and gives it back to Henry to use as a fake cover in which to carry his Official Army Military Manual stolen from the British army.

These are all books by women and books about slaves. Granny Nash's reading reflects a whole world of insurrection, rebellion, resistance, cries and campaigns for independence. It's another parallel story, set beside Henry's own story of resistance and Ireland's history of the struggle for independence. Through reading, the dispossessed are repossessed.

And that goes for Doyle's novels too. He listens to the voices of his characters so that we can also hear them. You will see in the interview included here that Doyle speaks of the ways in which language changes rapidly all the time. It evolves and reshapes everywhere, but this is especially so in Ireland where a love of words and stories is a kind of national characteristic. So history – which is words and stories – metamorphoses around us and we change with it.

You will see also in the interview that Doyle (gently) takes us to task for suggesting that *A Star Called Henry* is a departure from his earlier work because it is an historical novel. No, he said, that past is still present, in his own grandfather's life, in his own life, in the fact that Henry Smart – wherever he is – is still alive.

We will have to wait to find out where Henry is in the follow-up to *A Star Called Henry*, as Doyle has promised that he will continue his story. Perhaps we will also find out Miss O'Shea's first name. And we wonder if she too is still alive.

Not that it matters much, for Doyle is right. The point is that the characters are alive, and their children and their children's children are alive, and their stories will continue. Doyle's world may be peopled with imaginary characters but they reflect aspects of the real world. What his work tells us is that imaginative recognition of the existence of other lives, in other places, is essential for the recognition of sameness and the tolerance of difference. It is also the first stage of love.

Interview with Roddy Doyle

Dublin: 3 September 2003

MR: You often rely heavily on the use of dialogue. How much does it matter that you get the voice of the character absolutely right?

RD: It's very important. When I started my first novel, *The Commitments*, I realised that I wasn't going to spend much time describing the outward appearance of characters or observing them from a distance. And I almost immediately fell on the dialogue. I think on the second page or so I realised that the dialogue was going to be vital, so I spent a long, long time experimenting with the dialogue and deciding on the compromises that were needed between conveying working-class Dublin speak and, at the same time, allowing people to read it without having to halt and stop and wonder what was being said. So a lot of the rules that I set myself would have been in that first couple of pages of *The Commitments*. And I realised as well pretty quickly – as I would have done as somebody with a working set of ears, but I'd never given it too much thought – that within the general speech of an area every individual has his quirks or her quirks and words that they stress very often, and hesitancies, and I tried to incorporate them into the individual speech of characters. With *The Commitments*, because it was so dialogue-bound, by the time I was finished, I knew what I was doing.

Getting to know a character then in the later novels – because the later novels are narrated by the central characters – it's more complex, more demanding, and a very slow process. Really what you try to achieve is the creation of the character partly by what they talk about, what they write about, what their story is, and what their problems and triumphs are. But under all that you must convince the reader that you are reading the words of these people, and that takes time. So *The Woman Who Walked Into Doors* took two years to write and very little was written in the first year, it was more experimentation.

MR: When were you aware of your own voice, your own style being established? Was *The Commitments* the first thing you'd written?

RD: *The Commitments* wasn't the first thing. I started writing, on and off, in about 1982. I wrote *The Commitments* in 1986. I wrote a novel which, in retrospect, I realise was very poor. But I look back on it now and I suppose it was like a form of apprenticeship, getting things out of my system, experimenting. I was just pleased at the time – I think it was 1985 – that I'd finished it. I sent it off to every publisher's name I could find and it was rejected, or it never came back, and in the meantime I got working on *The Commitments*. I do remember clearly, very early on, getting quite giddy about *The Commitments* and thinking that something had clicked, and that this was actually what I really did want to write about and that this was what I knew about. I was a big fan of music and the idea of researching music was such a thrill – this was the kind of music I listened to all the time, and these were the characters that I really wanted to write about. It wasn't that I came from their particular place or that I knew them intimately (though actually I think I did), or that I was limited to that place. It just felt right. I didn't know whether there was writing like it out there, or whether other Dubliner writers had been doing it, or the Scottish or Welsh or English equivalents . . . I didn't know, but it felt fresh to me.

Then something clicked. I thought, 'Yeah, this is it. This is what I should be doing.'

MR: Why did you name the band 'The Commitments'?

RD: I'm not all that certain! It's tongue-in-cheek. They're committed to nothing really. I wanted, as Jimmy says he wanted, 'a good old-fashioned "the"'. That came out of . . . I think the late seventies, early eighties. There was that wonderful rush of punk bands who were all called 'the something or other'. You know, 'The Sex Pistols', 'The Clash', 'The Stranglers', 'The Specials' – all these great, great bands – 'Elvis Costello and *The* Attractions'. But then in the early eighties you had all these God-awful New Romantic bands reacting to the toughness of punk. And it wasn't as if they were more sophisticated, because they weren't, but they all had these awful bloody names – 'Spandau Ballet' and 'Duran Duran' – names that needed explaining. It was an in-joke that 'Duran Duran' was Milo O'Shea and the movie *Barbarella*, but it just wasn't worth explaining. And the music bore no relation whatsoever to the lunacy of *Barbarella*. 'A Flock of Seagulls' was another band I remember – just look at these idiots – and 'Kajagoogoo' was another. So Jimmy, like myself, was reacting to the pomposity and the shallowness of all that. Among other things he was just determined that his band was going to begin with a definite article, he was going to have no messing.

At first they were called 'The Partitions'. But I rejected that name quite early on. It seemed to make sense if it was a ska band, I don't know why, but if I was managing a ska band I'd call them 'The Partitions'.

But 'The Commitments' – I liked the way it scanned. I liked the way it sounded. I liked the tongue-in-cheek quality about it. Jimmy builds politics around it and he gives them pep talks, like a good football manager does before sending his underdogs out to fight Manchester United – it just made sense. And it was fun.

MR: Now, as you've listed all those different names of different bands, it makes me realise the way that you love language, unpicking words, codes, jargon and dialect. How does this influence your use of language, or are you just having fun?

RD: Well, I am having fun, but I've always been intrigued by slang, particularly when I started teaching. Slang is fascinating – it's such an unrecognised form of creativity. Every street has its slang, every generation has its slang. Some words survive a couple of days among a couple of friends. Others grow and grow. In *The Commitments* there's a slang word for penis called 'gooter', which lasted a couple of months round about 1974 or 1975 when I was in school. Except for a couple of friends of mine who take out the word now and again just to remind us of when we were young, 'gooter' has disappeared. I put it into *The Commitments* just for fun, and there were all sorts of debates as to whether the word actually existed or not. There was a sort of an annoyance that I would use a word that didn't exist, yet it did exist.

Slang and the way people use language – it's intriguing. I love the way young kids speak just when they're conquering language, and they can say something in a very literal sense, that, strictly speaking, doesn't make grammatical sense – hence its humour – but at the same time is to the point in a much sharper way sometimes than the official way. I think in the official versions we often bypass strict meaning or go around it in a diplomatic way, whereas when kids talk – I'm talking about little kids when they start commanding the language – they, seemingly, misunderstand yet very often they don't misunderstand at all and get to the point much much quicker.

And in Ireland there is another grammar bubbling under the English grammar, it's the Irish grammar. And I'm no big fan of the Irish language, and I detested the way that it was inflicted upon me when I was in school. You were a failure if you failed Irish, and you could get any amount of marks in every other subject on the planet, but if you failed Irish you weren't a true Irish person. I've always hated that, but at the same time I've got to recognise that this grammar is bubbling under the English grammar, and the language, as we use it here in Ireland, is the richer for it. Perhaps it is also the same in Scotland or Wales. I'm reading *Brick Lane* at the moment by Monica Ali, and I love the way the characters speak – the creativity of the Bangladeshi women when they're chatting to each other, how they use the language, it's glorious. These middle-aged women are being as inventive – in their closed and small world – as their teenage kids are outside on the street.

So I've always loved listening to language, and as I started writing I began to realise that I can press home the locality of the characters by making them speak in a particular way.

MR: You also seem to be interested in the modes and rhythms of the speech too. In *The Commitments* you can hear the songs in your head as you read the words, and in *A Star Called Henry* there are whole passages which are like long poetic rhythmic improvisations or riffs. Do you ever read your work out loud to yourself?

RD: I used to. I did at first, but we're going back a bit, so it's 1986 we're talking about, and I think I did – if not very loud, because I was living in a bedsit and there were neighbours all around me and behind me and below me and above me. So I didn't get much of a chance to scream out my art! But the rhythm is vitally important. If we were to take a conversation between three working-class men outside and just transcribed it literally, it wouldn't have rhythm. Passages of it would, but there would be hesitancies that would be probably 'dot dot dot', or dashes, or something on the page, and it would be a bit difficult to cope with, a bit difficult to engross oneself in. Whereas, like Sean O'Casey and others, I'll quite happily make compromises, take short cuts, get characters to speak in such a way that has a rhythm which suits me, rather than actually mirrors reality. There's a meeting between the art and reality when I'm doing the dialogue, and the rhythm is vitally important.

With *The Commitments* it just seemed a good idea to quote lyrics from songs. I didn't realise that you had to pay for these things! It just seemed to make sense, and to integrate it into the Dublin language. It was fun. But on top of that, once you had the rhythm of the songs, and the gaps between the songs (particularly as the band were rehearsing and then going on stage), the action, as described – things going well and things going badly – also had the rhythm. It's a bit like a well-cut film. In a well-cut film, the film will tally with the soundtrack, or the soundtrack will tally with the film. So, with *The Commitments* the narration had to be as rhythmic as the songs. I spend a lot of my time when I'm writing rejecting words because there's one syllable too many, or rejecting a sentence because it seems not to fit with the rhythm of the other sentences. I think it's one of the basic rules. If you're describing serenity, or whatever, the rhythm of the sentence is going to be different from the rhythm of a sentence describing anxiety. It's with experience that you realise that's actually true. You punctuate the sentence more severely if it's anxiety or fear or something like that.

I think the first book wrote itself. And it's only in retrospect that I begin to realise, 'Ah, yeah, that's why I did that.' If I'm reading a book or a story and I feel that not enough effort has been put into the writing – or the editing – I feel let down. So I put a lot of thought into the editing. As much thought goes into the editing as into the actual writing.

MR: The Barrytown setting – what was it about the particularity of that setting that made it so alive for you?

RD: Well, it was home in a way. As I visualised it, it was the place that I was teaching in. I didn't live there any more, though I lived quite close for convenience sake, about three miles nearer the city centre, in about the early to mid 1980s. The public housing estate that I began to visualise was more or less the same estate that I was looking at out of the window. My parents lived on the edge of that estate, and I watched it while I was growing up. So it had a certain settled quality to it because people had been living there for twenty-odd years, still with youngish families, children in their teens and younger, relatively few of them grown up. The trees and the hedges had grown, but a lot of the pavements had never been finished. The Chinese takeaway would last a couple of weeks and then become an Indian takeaway, and something else would open and shut. The hairdresser changed name every three weeks. The pub was new, brand new. So there was a rawness to it as well – leaving aside all the unemployment and the economics of it – which is now, in a way, gone. There were still these metal boxes which were temporary shops where people in a square area would go and get their milk, their bread and their basic commodities. But they were basically containers with the front part taken off, they were there temporarily, but they were there for twenty-odd years.

I didn't feel a need to describe it in any street-by-street detail because these estates ring Dublin. Kilbarrack is on the coast where I come from, and you could go around Dublin following what is now the M50, the motorway that bypasses Dublin, and you see these estates all over the place. Some of them older, some of them younger. Big imposing church, big schools, well kept but modern insofar as they are all comprehensive schools and built to a design that was replicated all over. Public housing is public housing is public housing. The architecture might vary but the spirit and the energy and the highs and the lows are the same everywhere. And I felt it was going to be very, very typical.

Then, as I was going to write *Paddy Clarke*, a bit like an archaeologist or something, I knew the place before those houses were built. They were fields. I knew what was there, I remembered the farmhouses. So I saw the place being built. I felt very strongly a sense of home. I felt that if a character walked down a fictionalised version of this street, I wouldn't have to stop and ponder what they saw. I would know. Because I knew the streets intimately. And I never drew a map. I was never overconcerned about whether he turned left or right – I thought that would make it too local, too fastidious, and would rob it of its universality. There was a typical quality to it all, and a humour and a particularity to it that attracted me as well. But really it was the world I was looking at and seeing and smelling every day, so it was just very familiar.

MR: Just as the place is partly in your imagination and partly in reality, the characters seem to have the same qualities. They seem to live with you. Sharon simply walks up the stairs in *The Commitments* and then all of a sudden you return to her character in *The Snapper*. Also there's Paula, from *Family*, who then reappears in *The Woman Who Walked Into Doors*.

RD: Some of the characters linger and others don't. Some of them serve their purpose in my head and I don't see any fascination in going back. Paddy Clarke, surprisingly for some people, is really a character in which I have no interest what-soever. I've been asked, 'When are you going to write another Paddy Clarke? What did he do in his teenage years?' And I couldn't care less. It sounds quite brutal, but he was fictional – all the characters are fictional.

But for whatever reason, Paula is still bubbling away there. I wouldn't be surprised if somewhere along the line I write another book either narrated by her or observing her later on, to see how she's getting on. Sharon has one line in *The Commitments* – the poetic 'Go an' shite' I think is the actual line! – and it wasn't that I thought, 'Well, she's a magnificent character, I'll go back and write a book about her.' It's just that I felt, when I finished *The Commitments*, that I liked the style and I liked the world, and I liked Jimmy Rabbitte, and I thought there was potential in the glimpses of the family that they'd had, and I thought I'd like to write something more intimate. So I thought I'd tackle pregnancy as I saw it – as it was! – outside marriage, and the reality of it in working-class Dublin in the mid to late 1980s. I don't know why but I just chose Sharon. It just seemed that I could do something fresh, but continue with what I was doing with *The Commitments* because I'd enjoyed it so much. So she ended up having a book of her own. Then her father grew out of that really, and it was *The Snapper* that determined me to write *The Van*. That's the way it goes. Some characters seem to linger. Others don't.

Patterns seem to linger too. The way of telling a story seems to linger and seems to endure another telling. Or an image. In *The Woman Who Walked Into Doors* the image of her being hit the first time, I repeat it again and again at slightly different angles, with slightly different wording every time. I'm sure it is a significant moment in anybody's life – the first time they're hit by their partner – and it just seemed to bear repetition that didn't seem like repetition – it seemed like a retelling. Whereas if I'd done another part of her life and repeated it, it would have seemed repetitious. So it's a question again of editing decisions that seem to knit the story in ways that more conventional methods don't, I suppose.

MR: Can I ask you about structure? In your first three books the narrative is more or less chronological, although we do return to certain episodes, whereas with *Paddy Clarke* and *The Woman Who Walked Into Doors* the chronology is much more mixed up. Is that dictated by the character?

RD: In a way, yes. It would be true to say that the first three stories are by and large linear, it's A to Z really. With *Paddy Clarke* I didn't have a shape for the book at all. I think, in a way, this was a necessity. I don't like dwelling too much on my personal life (though everything I write is personal), but with *Paddy Clarke* what happened was that my life at the time dictated the eventual shape of the book. I was still teaching full-time at that point, and I became the father of one child, and then – seemingly overnight, but not exactly – another child. So my time, to put it mildly, was very limited and I'd try and grab an hour or so in the evening, once the kids were settled. I was very keen to write about this childhood from the point of view of the child. Largely because, after the birth of my first child, I began to think of my own childhood – I suppose anticipating his. I began to use this theme, and it suited me down to the ground because an awful lot of *Paddy Clarke* is little things, little observations he makes, and later on I integrated them and threw a lot of them out and then tried to create a book that wasn't linear – a book that was from the point of view of a child.

I suppose it's things like school that force a linear pattern into children's lives, but little kids don't differentiate between what is important and what is trivial. Everything is either

stunningly boring or absolutely fascinating and whether it's officially so or not is irrelevant. Gradually, late in the process of
writing that book, it took shape. And in a way it's chronological insofar as it's roughly a year of his life. But it meanders a
lot. It's a spiral, and the spiral gets smaller and smaller until
the very end where it's like a whirlpool and he is just swal-
lowed by this thing, this horrible reality that his parents'
marriage is breaking up. There are hints at it at the beginning
and gradually the hints become more than hints and it's a bare
blunt fact that he can't ignore. But initially the eventual shape
of the book was dictated by the amount of time I had to write
and what I was writing about. Then it just made sense. I seem
to recall printing out everything and having possible chapters
and bits and pieces all over the floor and trying to summarise
them, as I often do when I'm doing a screenplay and experimenting with this shape and that shape, and gradually I realised,
'Well, that's just a little passage for its own sake, it's never going
to make any sense,' and I threw stuff out. Whereas another
line sometimes, just placed – seemingly at random – between
two more substantial chapters, made a childlike sense that
brought you closer to the belief that this was a ten-year-old kid
telling the story, and not a thirty-four-year-old writing the book.

With *The Woman Who Walked Into Doors,* I tried to imagine
this woman sitting down to write for the first time and I was
pretty sure that she'd buy a copybook, or there'd be one left
over in the house. And she'd have a pen, a Bic biro, nothing
else. And that she'd do this in the little bit of time she had
available. I imagined a very intelligent person (although her
intelligence would be unrecognised even by herself), who was
also very, very strong. Despite the fact that she liked reading
and had a certain amount of books she would be, at the risk
of sounding dismissive, 'unread', in that she wouldn't be a
student of literature. Sitting down to tell her story she would
start at the beginning. And that's how I started it. And again

I began to feel 'no'. Would Paula, who wants to write about other things, start at the beginning of her life as if it's a memoir? I couldn't see her doing it, because she'd be more interested in getting to the core. And at the same time I couldn't imagine myself reading it. However well intentioned, it was going to be tedious. So I let myself write away. With an awful lot of the violent stuff I already knew what I was going to write, but I didn't write it to begin with. I wrote about her childhood, and spent a long time writing, if you like, 'a day in the life of Paula' – the cleaning work she did, collecting her son, playing with her son, contrasting the darkness and the light, the weaknesses and strengths, the alcoholism and the attention to her parenting.

Gradually, then, it struck me that the way she would tell the story would be on three parallel tracks: her distant past, her recent past and her present. Once I'd decided that, it was a question of apportioning all these stories in front of me and, again, throwing out a lot of stuff that didn't fit.

I think with experience and with more books under one's belt you tend to be more confident, more adventurous. In which case, I think they're better books for the fact that they're not told in a linear way.

MR: A lot of your characters end up in situations where they face their own powerlessness – because of other people's cruelty, or because they're afraid of something. Virtually everybody, now I think about it. Maybe the only person who is powerful is Henry Smart from *A Star Called Henry*.

RD: Yeah, but he has to get out of the country . . . It's hard to generalise. All the characters, in a way, are confronted by the reality of their isolation. They live in a society – and this isn't unique to Ireland, but in the case of Jimmy Rabbitte, his father, Sharon, Henry later on, Paula definitely – that has no interest in them whatsoever. They're not even statistics really.

They are officially, but it never goes beyond that. Unfortunately, it hasn't changed all that much. They live on the periphery. They look for themselves on the television and they're not there, so culturally they don't exist. They're rejected really and it's up to them to take this fact by the scruff and reject it. And Jimmy Rabbitte does it, as a young man with all this energy and the arrogance that, somehow or another, he's got. So he says in his own inimitable way, 'Fuck this, I'm not going to take that,' and he creates his own world. Sharon does the same thing. In a way working-class Dublin society in the 1980s is quite tolerant of the fact that she's pregnant, but at the same time it's not enough – she insists on her romantic version of what happened, to keep her self-respect intact. It's to make sure that whatever happens it will be on her conditions and not on those of society, including her parents. Henry declares war on – not Britain, as such – but society, again, on the way it's run, the way it's operated; he's managed to climb out of it but others have failed, including his brother and his mother.

But I do think that even though they sometimes fail in their endeavours, the mere fact that they're telling their stories is the triumph. If we go looking for Paula now, years after the book was published, she'll still be living in that house. She'll have fallen off the wagon a couple of times I'm sure, she'll probably look older than she should do, she'll have lost more teeth than a woman her age should do, she may not be personally happy, but she's still taking on society and there are daily triumphs and there are daily failures. I'd be confident that her kids are getting on fine, particularly the two younger ones. So it's just a day-to-day battle and I suppose the triumph is in the fact that they keep coming for more.

MR: In a way, then, history – what is considered 'real' history, official history – is set on one side in your novels. In *A Star Called Henry* there's the Easter Rising and the independence question is played out on the sidelines. In the Barrytown trilogy, when the Russian premier Gorbachev gets a little look-in, there is the sense that 'real' history is all on the margins and these other characters are the real world. Is that a kind of political point?

RD: It is. What is our knowledge of history? The French Revolution? We can name the five key players, then we go on to Napoleon, Napoleon versus Wellington, and it's all key people. When you see a well-made film or story you think, 'Jesus Christ, there are hundreds of thousands of people dying here . . .' I think maybe the First World War changed the way that history is depicted, because it's not about Kitchener. We have difficulty actually remembering key names – we know Kitchener, we know the Tsar, we know Kaiser Bill – but it's all about the trenches, it's about men dying, suffocating in mud, it's about gas, it's about the horror of it. I love oral history – Studs Terkel and other oral historians who have just sat in front of people with tape recorders, ordinary people who are now dead and wouldn't have been recorded but for him and other historians who have done the same type of thing all over the world. And I just love that type of history because it seems to me living, it seems to me like people I know, people next door who have grown up in the same conditions. They've had their stories recorded and been given dignity and an importance that otherwise wouldn't be there. You know, if the history of Ireland in the late twentieth, early twenty-first centuries is told it's going to be about the various Taoiseachs, it's going to be about Gerry Adams – important figures granted. But behind that, what's it going to say about the Nigerian guy walking by there, or the woman from Sierra Leone, or the Latvian couple who'd decided to come and live here, or the Irish girl with the Latvian man? When it comes to the *breathing* history, it's out there on the street.

Henry is this character who has no official existence. He's a foot soldier really, who realises after a while that he's expendable. Every soldier is expendable, but the people who gave him a gun and gave him the names of people to kill knew it. He did it. He's responsible. But at the same time, he thought he was part of it and in fact he wasn't really. He was doing it for them, it wasn't for him. They were going to divide out the country, this class of people – the lower-middle class, Jesuit-educated – they all had it apportioned, and still do. And if you looked at the official history of Ireland, you would swear there was never a farm labourer ever existed. You would swear they were all farm owners. We're talking about a relatively small group of people – in a way, admirable – who dictated what Ireland was going to look like and was going to be shaped like. It could have gone any way.

An uncle of my father's joined the army in 1914. It was the British army when he joined and it was the British army four years later. But he was a hero when he marched off. He was a traitor when he came home. Within those four years an awful lot happened.

It's extraordinary when you go deeper into it. We are told to think of Ireland as a nation of farmers, but in fact there were relatively few farmers and a hell of a lot of labourers working for those farmers. And yet it's as if they didn't exist when you read the history of the nineteenth century – even though you know it's admitted that a million people, perhaps, starved in the famine and a million emigrated. It's an extraordinary rewriting of history. Well, it wasn't even written – so it's an extraordinary *writing* of history that allows one class of people to give their versions. It's inevitable. But for years in Ireland the other versions of history weren't there and, in fact, still aren't. The whole countryside is dotted with labourers' cottages. We drive by them, and nobody wonders, 'Who lived in them?'

It's the same with Dublin. I still hear people who say, 'Oh, everybody went to Trinity.' They didn't. A couple of thousand people went to Trinity. Everybody else *didn't* go to Trinity. Or 'everybody' ate at this particular restaurant. Most people at the time had never been inside a restaurant. They hadn't a clue what a restaurant looked like. Except for the odd café where they'd get a cake and a cup of tea.

It's easy to get worked up. Which seems a bit silly. When you think of history, or today when you look at television, at the images that we're being given, or when you read something in quite a good newspaper like the *Irish Times*, the tone seems so remote. It's being directed by about fifty people. It bears no relation to what the rest of us do. Fair play to them. I don't resent it. But when somebody comes back in fifty years' time and looks at the *Irish Times*, they will have an incredibly warped view of what life was like in Ireland in the twenty-first century.

So when you look at history as it's officially given, and then see the reality, or another reality, the stuff of fiction begins to plonk itself right in front of you. And I've never been overly interested in leaders.

MR: What prompted you to move from a contemporary setting to a historical setting for *A Star Called Henry*?

RD: Well, *A Star Called Henry*, which probably in one or two bookshops is under historical fiction, is in fact not an historical book at all. It's written in the first person, so the narrator is still alive – or was when I was writing it and still is because I'm writing a second book by the same character. He's an astonishing age now, but he's still alive. So he's writing now, although about events that are now considered historical. It's not an historical novel as such because it's about a living human being writing about his past, granted, but living today. And then, I suppose, every society is much the same, but it's the one I'm familiar with – the political patterns that emerged from the war of Independence and the civil war, in the first two decades of the twentieth century, are still out there. The politics are a mystery really, certainly to British people, less so, I think, to the Americans – these two big parties, Fianna Fáil and Fine Gael can be seen as the Republicans and the Democrats – all dictated what went on. Decisions people made or didn't make.

When I was a child we visited a village that one of my aunts lived in in County Wexford and there was a shop that you went into and there was a shop that you very definitely didn't go into. They both sold the same products at the exact same price. But one of them had been on the right side during the civil war – which in the mid 1960s, when I would have been there, would have been forty years old, yet it was still a raw wound. And they'd been on the right side as far as my aunt was concerned, but the wrong side officially because it was the Republican side, the diehard side that lost the war. So we took our pennies and we spent them in that shop and we never went into the other one. On pain of severe punishment. It was like going into a Protestant church – the Devil would get you if you went into the Fine Gael shop.

It's still there. It's current affairs. There are still people who would be quite willing to plant bombs. They get their legitimacy from the Proclamation that was read out outside the GPO in 1916. The fact that again and again the vast majority of people in Ireland will reject violence and vote for a peaceful solution is still ignored, as their legitimacy comes from the Proclamation in 1916. But to understand it, you go back, and not too far back either. History's fascination is the fact that very often it isn't history at all, it's just current affairs.

MR: A lot of your characters do terrible things or end up in situations where their sense of themselves is compromised, situations in which they don't behave well. But you never judge them. Is that hard to do?

RD: Well, it's not hard to do. There's only one of them that murders people and that's Henry.

MR: There's Charlo in *The Woman Who Walked into Doors*.

RD: I try not to be judgemental because, with Charlo, I was writing from the point of view of a woman who loved him. If I were reading about him under cover of the newspapers I would be more judgemental.

In the case of Henry what I tried to imagine – and it was easy enough because there were memoirs written by very impressive people (one particularly by Ernie O'Malley) – was me at sixteen or seventeen in Dublin in 1916. Possibly I wouldn't have had a clue as to what was going on. I probably would have been a bit confused as to which side I wanted to win. I would have been a bit divided as to that. It would really have depended on where I lived or whether my father was doing what he did, as a printer, or later on as a civil servant – you know, which class he was in. How would I view what was going on? Would I see it as being revolution, or would I see it as being rebellion, or would I see it as being an inconvenience? I tried to imagine myself in a city which would have been much smaller, a walking city, with not remotely the same amount of traffic, and hearing the gunshots – which an awful lot of people did hear, because it was a lesson to the Irish people – of these men being executed, being shot, without trial, without proper authority, you know, the usual 'we'll teach these fuzzy-wuzzies a lesson'. Then I tried to imagine, if I was a young guy without attachments, without children, without responsibilities – would I have got involved? And there's a huge possibility that I, like hundreds of others, would have. And then, at what point does freedom fighting become murder? So I don't think Henry feels very guilty about what he's done but he decides that he's not going to do any more. In a way, guilt seems to me to be superfluous. Henry, by writing the book and by calling himself a 'complete and utter fuckin' eejit', as he does, is about as guilty as he's going to feel, and he's now going to try and live the rest of his life in a different way.

With Charlo [In *The Woman Who Walked Into Doors*], I was writing from the point of view of the woman who loves him. I don't think she veers away from the horror of what he does. She's more horrified, I think, by what he does to the other woman than what he did, for seventeen years, to her. It's one of those complicated things. She loves him. And love, in a way, is inexplicable. Why? You know the questions: why did you love this man? Why did you marry this man? There's no real answer to it. Why do people fall in love with patently unsuitable partners? It happens all the time and it will continue to happen.

The nice thing about fiction is that it's free. You don't have to judge. It's made up. So if somebody does something horrific, it's within the page. There are moral implications and things like that and the reader reacts to it as if it's real sometimes. But I suppose that as the writer of fiction, I can afford to give Charlo the space to be Charlo. Whereas if I were a juror, I'd want him off the streets pretty quickly. So there is a difference between being a fiction writer and a citizen. I do think murder is murder. But, for example, it's that moral, muddy area that they are in in Northern Ireland at the moment. A man, 1973, walks into a pub on a Friday night, leaves a briefcase in the pub, ten minutes later the briefcase explodes and dozens of people die, or are mutilated for the rest of their lives. To my mind he's a murderer. Twenty-five years later, in an attempt to end this repetitious violence, he has to be looked at across a table, and you have to look him in the eye, you have to address him and perhaps shake his hand, and it's not 'let bygones be bygones' but you have to see him as a human being. You have to recognise that the way to deal with this man is to release him, let him go, in this particular context. Don't execute him. Don't make a martyr of him. Let him go. Let him deal with his own demons, as an awful lot of them have done and are doing. Let him be carried shoulder-high through his own ghetto, or let him go on the run. Whatever it is. But there's a point where reality dictates – wise reality, if such a thing exists – that 'an eye for an eye, a tooth for a tooth' doesn't work that way. It's not good science. It's not good morality. It's not good politics. It's not good day-to-day living. So I think, in a way, as a writer of fiction, I can get closer to these horrible realities.

Everybody has their awful, hangover, embarrassing stories. It's the small things that often make people cringe, much more than murder does. In a film or on a page, somebody getting sick when they shouldn't get sick, somebody breaking wind when they shouldn't break wind or doing the most inappropriate things, makes people gag, in a way that murder might not. It's all a bit haphazard.

But fiction has many purposes. And one of them is that it allows the writer to get closer to people that he or she isn't, and maybe present them to others. I'm not trying to humanise Charlo, but I think it's important that he's a human being, always, and that he's never a stereotypical rogue – he is that, but he's also a human being. He must be a human being. If he's not, it makes a nonsense of Paula's emotions. So he has to be living. He has to have a charm. There has to be a reason why she falls in love with him. Whatever it is. His appearance, his walk, the way he smokes – all these things make a human being out of him.

MR: You have said that fiction should challenge a reader – even intimidate them. Why do you think that?
RD: Well . . . it's a personal thing really. Having started writing about working-class people, and really I suppose I haven't written about much else, there are official ways that you are

supposed to write about working-class people, and the first challenge is to get rid of that. And if these people say 'fuck', then let them say 'fuck'. And if others say, 'Oh, they're inarticulate,' you can spend the rest of your life saying, 'No, they're not inarticulate, it's just that it happens to be that "fuck" is in the rhythm of the language: fuckin' this, fuckin' that . . . it doesn't mean that they can't say anything else, it's just the pattern of their language.' And you can go on and on, but the wise thing to do is just ignore it and keep on writing.

You're challenging preconceived notions of what working-class people are like, or should be like. If the accusation is there that they're drunk all the time, or that they're fat, or whatever, just ignore it and get on with it and just do what you think is true. You're challenging preconceived notions about the working class. They're coming from the left, they're coming from the right.

When *The Family* was broadcast, jeez, the objections came from all sorts of quarters about how 'it wasn't representative'. And the last thing a fiction writer should do is try to be representative. If you're writing about a serial killer and are worried about 'oh, I'd better not have him do that because I don't want to upset serial killers all over the world', or their spouses. You put on these blinkers to an extent, and don't allow these preconceived notions in – or you can play with them, but don't allow them to dictate what you're writing about.

So there's the challenge. Within a book like *A Star Called Henry* there's the challenge of giving history in a different way. Challenging the notions that – as somebody who was educated in the sixties and seventies – were taken to be fact, and rewriting them and playing with them. Mocking with things that, in Ireland, are almost religious and unquestionable. The feeling that what happened in 1916 was *good*, and it couldn't be questioned.

In the case of *The Woman Who Walked Into Doors*, I think

women who'd been through the same experiences were quite impressed with the accuracy of it. But I did get quite a lot of 'why didn't she leave him?' objections. The objection was from middle-class people particularly – and I'm not underestimating the pain or the difficulty of a middle-class life – but they refused to get beyond their own circumstance. For example, their ability to drive a car, their ownership of a car, a joint account, money of their own perhaps, skills, things like this which Paula doesn't have at all. Whereas they might. And again, I think, going to the door and making the last big step out of the door is always very difficult. But whereas they might have done it, they couldn't see that it's much more difficult for somebody without the bits of power that they had. And again, you just keep on writing and doing what you think is true. Cheerfully so in most cases.

In a way it's a knowledge as well. You can tell a story well. But you're telling a story on top of a tradition that goes back thousands of years. If you want to tell the story, surely, there's a way of telling it that's a bit different. A way of telling it that challenges, plays with chronology, plays with the point of view, or goes for the point of view of somebody who never had a point of view before. Rather than just be a slave to a tradition, which is often lazy, or a slave to other people's preconceived notions of what it should or shouldn't be like – just do what you want to do.

If I was writing about a more middle-class life – that solid generation, that old middle-class life – the temptation would be to sneer at it. I think that temptation is always there. I think that that temptation is also there among the people who come from just that background, and want to get the wildness of their youth out of the way, and yet will go straight back in and send their kids to the same poxy schools that they were sent to. The tendency would be to sneer. I think that if I were to write about that life I would go out of my way *not* to sneer. I would try to be as respectful of it as I have been, I think, of working-class life.

I'm not going to write about [middle-class life] because I don't know enough about it and I'm not really interested. But I think you can entertain, I think you can entertain and challenge and provoke at the same time. Without going out of your way just to shock, for the sake of shock.

VINTAGE
LIVING
TEXTS

The Barrytown Trilogy

IN CLOSE-UP

Reading guides for

THE COMMITMENTS

BEFORE YOU BEGIN TO READ . . .
— Read the interview with Doyle. You will see there that he
identifies a number of themes and techniques in this novel:

- Setting
- Rhythm and pace
- Character and voice
- Identity and pride

Other themes and techniques that may be useful to consider
while reading the novel include:

- Self-creation
- Commitment
- Politics
- Music
- The idea of the trilogy

Reading activities: detailed analysis

Focus on: the title

EXPLORE THE CONNOTATIONS . . .

— The title of this first novel in *The Barrytown Trilogy* is taken from the name that Jimmy Rabbitte gives to the rock and soul group whom he offers to manage. Remember this as you read. Is there any specific moment when 'The Commitments' makes sense in terms of the values and allegiances that Jimmy suggests should be important to the group and their music? Doyle discusses this topic in the interview (pp. 15–16).

— Then think about 'commitment'. What does the term suggest to you? To whom or what should one be 'committed', And why? How might this relate to what happens in the course of the story? Who is committed to what and how a) at the beginning of the story, and b) by the end of the novel?

Focus on: beginnings

ASK YOURSELF . . .

— Doyle dedicates his first novel to his parents. Authors often use quotes from literature or philosophy to give authority to their dedications. Doyle uses a quote from one of his own characters. What effect does this have on your attitude to the

dedication? Is it devalued because it invokes, for emphasis, the medium of fiction? Or is the sentiment heightened because the author has created not only the dedication but also its reinforcing quote and the character who offers that quotation?
— You might also consider the effect the quotation has on the status of the book. Could it be seen to place the novel on a par with great works of literature?

RESEARCH, CONSIDER AND COMPARE . . .
— What purpose do epigraphs serve? Why might an author use one? Why might an author not use one? What does the use of the James Brown epigraph say about the novel? Compare the epigraph here to the one Doyle uses in *The Woman Who Walked Into Doors*:

> At the age of 37 –
> She realised she'd never ride –
> Through Paris –
> In a sports car –
> With the warm wind in her hair –
>
> Shel Silverstein, '*The Ballad of Lucy Jordan*'

— This tone of regret and lost opportunity permeates the novel. What can be said about James Brown's song 'Superbad'? Note how Doyle uses lyrics in *The Commitments*? What quality do lyrics have that other easily quotable sources might not have? How many of these songs do you recognise? How many of the tunes can you remember?

SECTION I
(pp. 7–15)

Focus on: the theme of identity

EXAMINE . . .

— Look at the interaction between the characters. What do you notice about the roles each one takes? What does the opening line of this section say about the book as a whole? On p. 11 Jimmy Rabbitte tries to assess *why* Derek and Outspan and Ray might want to form a band. He says, 'Yis want to be different, isn't tha' it? Yis want to do somethin' with yourselves, isn't tha' it?' Ask yourself how far this is Jimmy's focus – that is, on being different, standing out, making a statement. Do Outspan and Derek feel the same way? Is there a difference between what they say about their wish to be different and how they act? Work through each of their responses to the questions that Jimmy asks.

— At the end of the section, the band define themselves in several ways. They ask, 'What are we Jimmy?' They are given a name – 'The Commitments' – and a definition – 'Dublin soul'. What do these definitions mean for the band? Are there any hints in the defining process as to the band's future? How does Jimmy's *Hot Press* advertisement on p. 15 further set out the band's remit?

CONSIDER . . .

— Look at Jimmy's speech on p. 13. This is one of Doyle's best-known statements. Throughout the rest of the novel the characters use racist terms and display very old-fashioned attitudes towards their role models, the black soul singers. However, they see themselves as following a tradition of escape from oppression, and indeed consider themselves proud to be 'black'. Keep this in mind as you read the novel, being aware of what inspires the band and whether this vision changes. In particular, keep a note of any racist remarks and how they contrast with the admiration that the band feel for Motown and soul singers – who also happen to be black. Look, for instance, at the gang's reaction to the picture of Marvin Gaye in a suit (p. 40).

ANALYSE . . .

— As Jimmy makes his speech the text gives Derek and Outspan's reactions – or lack of them – in parentheses. Analyse the technical effects resulting from this method. On the one hand it suggests the fact that only one person is doing the thinking here. On the other it provides a parallel text for Jimmy's voice. Then again it implies an audience for Jimmy both inside the text (Derek and Outspan) and outside the text (us, the readers).

Focus on: rebellion

EXPLORE . . .

— What do you think that Jimmy hopes to achieve with 'The Commitments'? How might this be construed as an act of rebellion or revolution?

SECTION 2
(pp. 15–30)

Focus on: language and humour

EVALUATE . . .

— Take a note of the repetition of certain words, for example 'cunt' and 'fuck'. Why does Doyle – or his characters – use them so often? What effect is produced by the frequent use of them? Does the reader become desensitised to them? Do the words themselves become a barrier to the development of the characters, or are they irrelevant to the reading process?

ASSESS . . .
— Would you describe the technical use of swear words as realistic, or stylised?

FIND . . .
— In this section, find some examples of how the use of sexual swear words becomes the basis of humour. Often they are used as interjections, or for emphasis. At other times they become instrumental in the conversation for their own merits. Humour can be created by the subversion of this social norm – for example, when Deco says 'Funk off' to Jimmy on p. 20. Find other examples of the complicated relationship these characters have with 'bad' language.

COMPARE . . .
— If you go on to read *The Snapper*, the next part in *The Barrytown Trilogy*, you will see that there is a running gag around the fact that Jimmy Sr and the children swear regularly, while Veronica tries to tick them off. Compare that use of 'bad' language with what goes on in *The Commitments*.

Focus on: characterisation

LIST . . .
— List the characteristics of each member of 'The Commitments'. Note the strengths and weaknesses that are immediately obvious. Are there any that they all share? Joey The Lips Fagan is obviously different from the rest. How does this help or hinder him in his relationship with the other members of the band? How does his difference from the others help or hinder the band as a whole? How and why does Jimmy react to Joey?

45

SECTION 3
(pp. 30–45)

Focus on: dialogue and character

CONSIDER . . .

— Doyle's writing has been criticised for its lack of description. It has been said that he relies too heavily on his particular style of dialogue, leaving his work in a no-genre-land between novel and drama. What do you think? What information is given about what the characters look like, where they live and rehearse, how they feel? Is this enough? How would the novel be different if there were more description?

MAKE UP . . .

— Write a fifty-word description of the physical appearance of ONE of the following characters: Imelda, Joey The Lips Fagan, Jimmy, Declan. How much have you imagined? How much have you sourced in the text itself? What does this tell you about your own relationship to the text as a reader?

COMPARE . . .

— How would you describe the way Doyle writes conversation? Pick up a book from your bookshelf; almost any realist novel will do. Compare the style of dialogue in your chosen novel with that of *The Commitments*. Doyle's way of writing dialogue differs from the usual style. How? Note features such as punctuation and orthography – what the words look like on the page – as well as what is said. What effect does this style have on the pace and energy of the novel? Does it matter that the reader does not always know exactly who is speaking? How does this style relate to the action of the novel? How does it affect the question of the lack of descriptive prose?

Focus on: names and naming

ASSESS . . .

— In the early pages of the novel Jimmy reveals his insecurity about using his own name for professional purposes. He does not consider it appropriate – 'Yeh never heard of a millionaire bein' called Jimmy' (p. 23). He needs a different persona to suit his ambition.

— How does the band react to the idea of having stage names? Who gives them their names, and what significance does this have? How does each of their names reflect on their personalities? Are there any names that are more ironic than descriptive? The characters are proud of their names. What do they mean to the individual members? At the end of the section, Joey The Lips Fagan names Jimmy. How does this solidify the importance of the naming ceremony?

Focus on: racism

LOOK BACK . . .

— Look back at Jimmy's speech on p. 13 about the Irish being 'the niggers of Europe'. Now look at the section on pp. 43–4 about Outspan's name. It is condemned as 'racialist'. Why? Consider the implications of linking these two passages.

THEN ASK YOURSELF . . .

— Consider the following story. During the 1970s when Nelson Mandela was in prison and the black Inkatha Freedom Party were attempting to overthrow the white rulers and government of South Africa and to do away with the system of apartheid (whereby legal and social constraints decreed the ways in which blacks should be segregated from whites in all public areas, where they may live and go to school, how they might travel and with whom they might have relationships), many European countries – including Britain – operated a boycott against South

Africa. Free trade was not allowed, diplomatic missions were withdrawn, no friendly exchange – including touring cricket teams, for instance – were permitted, and people were encouraged to boycott the purchase of South African goods.

At this time a white liberal woman, opposed to apartheid, goes into a greengrocer's in Edinburgh. She wants to buy some oranges, but before she decides which ones she will purchase she asks the shopkeeper where the oranges are from. 'South Africa,' comes the reply. 'In that case,' the customer says, 'I won't buy them.' 'Och,' says the shopkeeper, 'I don't blame you. All those dirty black hands all over them . . .'

Where does the humour in this story lie? Is it funny at all? Or is it sad?

Looking over Sections 1–3

QUESTIONS FOR DISCUSSION OR ESSAYS

1. 'I'm black an' I'm proud' (p. 13). Consider the implications of this statement for Jimmy Rabbitte and the members of 'The Commitments'.

2. Discuss the effect of Doyle's choice of language and how this affects the reader's reactions.

3. '*The Commitments* is a novel about sex and politics.' Discuss.

SECTION 4
(pp. 45–64)

Focus on: writing style

DO IT YOURSELF . . .
— This novel contains renditions of several soul and Motown

songs. Despite the lack of sound, Doyle writes these songs as if they were being sung. How does he do this? Does it work?
— Listen to a song that you like and write down the lyrics. Pay attention to the accent of the singer and any regional dialects you hear. Now look at the songs in this section. Listen to one of the songs written down here. Sing along with it using the words on the page as a guide. Does it help? Try singing with a Dublin accent – the text should help.

Focus on: power relations

ANALYSE . . .
— In this section Joey The Lips takes charge of rehearsals and the band. He is seen to be a leader and a role model. How is this demonstrated in the text? Who else holds the group together? What are the different ways these characters influence the others? In this section it becomes clear that sexual relations, as well as being a unifying influence, have the potential to split the group. How do Jimmy's three influences of music, politics and sex interact, and what kind of power relations do they create within the group?

ASK YOURSELF . . .
— Is there any other thing or things that gives Joey the edge over the other characters? Use this list to help you: good looks, age, knowledge, skill, money, a place of his own, family relations, knowing important people, size, style.

Focus on: narrative structure

EXPLAIN . . .
— Look at how this novel constructed? How is it broken down? How is the passage of time indicated? What makes it different from other novels? What does this do to the way you read?

MAKE A TIME PLAN . . .

— Look over what you have read of the novel so far and map out a chronology showing how many pages cover each episode in real (or rather fictional) time.

— Then think about how often an episode is revisited. Do any of the characters recall things that have happened in the past? If they do, how and why might that be significant?

SECTION 5
(pp. 64–99)

Focus on: idiom

COMPARE . . .

— Look at the alterations Deco makes to the songs he sings. This is his way of making the songs his own. He creates Dublin soul. Take note of the choices he makes when doing this. In 'Night Train' (pp. 91–3) he reverses the usual hierarchy of towns by naming the working-class suburb of Kilbarrack 'the home o' the blues', while the exclusive Sutton is 'where the rich folks live', later changed to 'where the snobby bastards live' (p. 126). In doing this, he creates a community out of his audience by including them in the band's act, claiming a social and artistic affinity with them. On a wider level, Doyle does the same thing with the book itself. By using 'Dublinese', which can sometimes seem impenetrable to those who do not know the area or the accent, he makes his community the exclusive one. Compare this novel with others that rely heavily on idiom, for example Toni Morrison's *Beloved* (1987) or Meera Syal's *Life Isn't All Ha Ha Hee Hee* (2001). What do these novels have in common? What are they trying to achieve by using this stylistic device? Do they succeed?

Focus on: humour

ASSESS . . .

— 'The Commitments'' first gig is painfully funny to read about. Much of the humour in it comes from pathos – when expectations are built up towards a climax which is ruined. A good example of this is at the beginning of the gig, on p. 85:

> This was it. Even if there were only thirty-three in the hall. James Brown had played to less. Joey The Lips said so.
> —Ladies an' gentlemen, Jimmy said to the mike.
> There was a cheer, a big one too, from the other side of the curtain.
> —Will yeh please put your workin' class hands together for your heroes. The Saviours o' Soul, The Hardest Workin' Band in the World, ——Yes, Yes, Yes, Yes——The Commitments.
> He dropped the mike and pulled the cord. The curtain stayed shut.
> —Wrong rope, son, said the caretaker.
> —Yeh fuckin' sap, said Imelda.

— What other types of humour can you find in this section? How much of the humour relies on the interaction between the audience (of thirty-three and Mickah) and the band themselves?

Looking over Sections 4–5

QUESTIONS FOR DISCUSSION OR ESSAYS

1.   'Doyle writes the music of the soul of Dublin.' Discuss.

2.   Could *The Commitments* be called a drama in novel form?

3. 'Humour in *The Commitments* lies only in the exploitation of badly spoken working-class caricatures who have little ambition and less chance of ever succeeding.' Do you agree with this statement?

SECTION 6
(pp. 99–124)

Focus on: gender politics

ANALYSE . . .

— Look at the roles played by women in this novel. Are they as important as the men? The Commitmentettes have two purposes – looking good on stage and being attractive to the band. In this section Jimmy realises that Imelda is central to the band's success – not because of her talent or social skills, but because the men all fancy her (p. 124).

— Can you find other examples of gender inequality? Can you find any where the men are taken advantage of? Does this inequality reflect badly on the author, or do you think it is an accurate representation of attitudes in the music world? The book was published in 1987. Do you think the balance would be different if it were being written now? Are there any examples of times when a sexist attitude works in someone's favour? Are there any characters who subvert gender stereotyping?

ASSESS . . .

— The band perform 'It's a Man's World' on pp. 116–17. How does this particular song contribute to the gender debate going on in the novel at this point?

Focus on: the theme of identity

EVALUATE . . .

— In this section one member of the band asserts his growing sense of his own identity. Who is it and how does he do this? What does this mean for the novel as a whole? Consider why this self-assertion is problematic for the other members of the band. What does this say about their own sense of identity?

— Reread Jimmy's manifesto on p. 11. How have his attitudes changed? Why? In this section music could be seen as a metaphor for lifestyle. How have the characters' attitudes to life changed during the course of the novel so far?

REVIEW . . .

— Deco upsets the band by failing to introduce them properly by their stage names (p. 102). Why does this matter so much to them? What do their stage names represent? Reread pp. 40–5 and see if their significance has changed.

SECTION 7
(pp. 124–32)

Focus on: highs and lows

TRACE . . .

— Write out a plan of the band's activities for the evening, including the successes of the gig, the response to the Dublin version of 'Night Train', Jimmy's negotiations with Eejit Records, and the break-up of the band. Examine each action. Are there any that are unpredictable? Examine Jimmy's conversation with Dave from Eejit. What are his priorities here and what are Dave's priorities? Why does the band split up? Are these factors hinted at through the text? Compare the end of this section with the start of the novel. Can you see any similarities, and anything that has fundamentally changed?

SECTION 8
(pp. 132–40)

Focus on: characters

ANALYSE . . .

— Look at the conversations Jimmy has in this section. Joey reveals that he can't live a life without soul, so he needs to go back to America. But Jimmy has his doubts about Joey's story. Together with the information Imelda gives him about Joey's reaction to the possibility of her pregnancy, a new side of Joey's personality is revealed.

— First of all, ask yourself how this changes your attitude to Joey. Then think about how this information makes you reassess Jimmy's attitude to Joey. And what about the rest of the band? How does this make you rethink your assessment of the way the band looked up to Joey?

— Does this new information about Joey affect the way you view certain aspects of the novel? Does it say anything about the medium of fiction? And what does this suggest in terms of the fact that Doyle uses Joey's words to dedicate the novel to his parents? What does the quote say now about the novel, or the character, or the sentiment?

— Finally, does Jimmy's conversation with Imelda shed a different light on the questions raised about gender politics in Section 6?

COMPARE . . .

— Compare the last page of the novel with the first section. What has changed? Compare the ideologies of the two groups.

How have 'The Brassers' learned from their experience as 'The Commitments'? Compare the two names – how do they illustrate this development? Look again at the power relations in the first section. Do you think this change will have an effect on the future of 'The Brassers'?

RESEARCH AND COMPARE . . .
— Look at the ways in which bands are set up today. Find out what you can about the formation of The Beatles. Find out what you can about the formation of the Spice Girls. What is the difference between the two? In what kind of room did The Beatles begin? Do you know? And the Spice Girls? How public was each of these events?
— How does this compare with the ideological basis for 'The Commitments', and the more commercial configuration of 'The Brassers'. You may be familiar with the film *This is Spinal Tap*. If so, where do you think 'The Commitments' fit in between 'Spinal Tap' and today's pop groups?

Looking over Sections 6–8

QUESTIONS FOR DISCUSSION OR ESSAYS
1. 'Joey The Lips Fagan was a fake, therefore "The Commitments" soul was fake.' Discuss.

2. 'They are the same people playing the same songs.' Are 'The Commitments' and 'The Brassers' the same band?

3. 'The women in this novel are useful only for looking pretty and filling in the backing track.' 'The Commitmentettes hold 'The Commitments' together, and then break them apart. They seem to play inconsequential roles, but the story is theirs more than anybody else's.' Which of these statements is the more accurate?

Looking over the whole novel

QUESTIONS FOR DISCUSSION OR ESSAYS

1. 'Once you've understood the language, you have understood the whole of *The Commitments*.' Discuss.

2. Make a case for any ONE of the following characters as the central focus of *The Commitments*: Jimmy, Joey, Imelda, Declan.

3. Describe your idea of 'Dublin soul'.

4. What is the function of the songs in the novel?

5. 'Yis want to be different, isn't tha' it?' (p. 11). How far is this the key idea in the novel?

6. Consider how Jimmy's manifesto on p. 13 relates to the themes of the novel as a whole.

7. Why is the Dublin setting so important to *The Commitments*?

8. Choose any passage from the text and work through the ways in which rhythm and pace function in the novel.

9. '*The Commitments* is a novel about identity.' Discuss.

10. In what ways is 'commitment' the principle theme of the novel?

Reading guides for

THE SNAPPER

BEFORE YOU BEGIN TO READ . . .
— Read the interview with Doyle. You will see there that he identifies a number of themes and techniques that are discussed in his novel. These themes include:

- Setting
- Character and voice
- Identity and pride

Other themes that may be useful to consider while reading the novel include:

- Self-creation and power
- Words and meaning
- The family
- Fathers
- Continuity

Reading activities: detailed analysis

Focus on: the title

EXPLORE THE CONNOTATIONS . . .

— To what does 'the snapper' refer? What or who is 'the snapper'? As you read over the novel, bear the title in mind and look for any helpful allusions or references that you can link to the title.

— When you have got to the end, look over your list of references and think again about the title. It is specific to the circumstances of the plot, but what larger metaphoric or thematic relevance can you discern? (There is one such passage on p. 205.) Note that you won't find an exposition of 'theme' or 'relevance' in the text itself – that meaning is unsaid, and you have to tease it out for yourselves.

Focus on: the centre and the margins

LOOK BACK . . .

— If you have read Doyle's *The Commitments* you will know that Sharon had a walk-on part in that book. Find the reference. A warning – it is tiny – she is someone who is briefly met on the stairs and who then disappears.

— How do you feel about the fact that Sharon – a character on the sidelines – is here reintroduced as the heroine? In setting up a portrait of her in your imagination, how are you helped now by knowing what you do from your reading of *The Commitments* – about her life, her family, her brother, her setting?

ASK YOURSELF . . .
— Consider what kinds of political (in the widest sense) point may be made by this transfer of a character from the margins to the centre. Doyle says something about this in the interview, refer back to it for more help with this issue.

SECTION I
(pp. 145–52)

Focus on: beginnings

CONSIDER . . .
— This novel begins with a question. Jimmy Sr then asks several other questions. Which one is the important one? How does this effect of question – and, often, of no answer – encourage you to go on reading? Do you want to go on reading? Why exactly?

COMPARE . . .
— Think about the opening lines of some well-known books. Examples might include:

- 'It is a truth universally acknowledged, that a single man in possession of a good fortune, must be in want of a wife.' Jane Austen, *Pride and Prejudice* (1813)
- 'I shall not say why and how I became, at the age of fifteen, the mistress of the Earl of Craven.' Harriette Wilson, *Memoirs* (1825)
- 'There was no possibility of taking a walk that day.' Charlotte Brontë, *Jane Eyre* (1847)

- 'It was the best of times, it was the worst of times . . .' Charles Dickens, *A Tale of Two Cities* (1859)
- 'With this drop of ink at the end of my pen I will show you . . .' George Eliot, *Adam Bede* (1859)
- 'Mrs. Dalloway said she would buy the flowers herself.' Virginia Woolf, *Mrs Dalloway* (1925)
- 'The past is a foreign country: they do things differently there.' L. P. Hartley, *The Go-Between* (1953)
- 'Like most people I lived for a long time with my mother and father.' Jeanette Winterson, *Oranges Are Not the Only Fruit* (1985)
- 'We slept in what had once been the gymnasium.' Margaret Atwood, *The Handmaid's Tale* (1987)
- 'I was told by a Guard who came to the door.' Roddy Doyle, *The Woman Who Walked into Doors* (1996)

— In what ways does the opening of *The Snapper* differ from these? Make a list. When you have read the novel to the end, think again about your list and consider the ways in which the clues that you acquired here on the opening page gave an indication of what kind of novel was to come.

Focus on: annunciation and revelation

REFLECT . . .

— Think about the piece of information that Sharon is offering to her parents, and the information that she is denying them.

— Then look up a passage in the New Testament: Luke, 1:26–38. When you have read the story in the Bible, consider how it might connect to Sharon's story. In what ways is it the same? What is different? Is this a useful comparison? What might it suggest?

— The scene in the New Testament where the Angel Gabriel appears to Mary is called the 'Annunciation', or the 'announcement' and it has been portrayed by many artists in the last two thousand years, including Raphael, Titian, Botticelli and – more recently – Paula Rego. Look up any such image – you will find some on the Internet. Note that, even where these pictures are very grand, they often include some attention to domestic detail. Make a list of those elements in your chosen picture. Then look again at this passage and see how many modern equivalents you can find in this modern scene of 'annunciation'.

THEN QUESTION . . .

— Doyle's writing has often been described as 'realistic' or about 'the commonplace'. In the light of the comparisons you have just made, would you say that this was all they are, or is there something else?

Focus on: language

ASSESS THE IDIOM . . .

— As with all *The Barrytown Trilogy*, most of the text is made up of dialogue; not just that, but a special and particular style of dialogue in a localised dialect and idiom. Look up the difference between 'idiom' and 'dialect' and 'accent' and 'slang' and 'catchphrases'. Then look over this section and write down all the words that you find odd. Note: if you are reading this in Dublin, you may find none of it odd – or, on the other hand, you might, because some slang words will have passed out of currency. If you are reading this in Canada, you'll probably find a great many words odd. Write them down. Include the ones you know, but which may have changed meaning, and the ones you don't know. Examples might include: snotty, a wobbler, fair play to yeh, eejit, after hittin' me, queer, the gear he wears, louser.

— How does this language help to create the scene and setting of the novel?

Focus on: parents and children

ASK YOURSELF . . .
— Read to the end of the scene. Try to work out Jimmy Sr's shifting reactions to Sharon's news. What different emotions does he experience? What is – essentially – his underlying attitude to Sharon? Does that change at all here or is it still the same by the end of the scene?

SECTION 2
(pp. 152–68)

Focus on: narrative technique

ANALYSE . . .
— Look over the smaller scenes that make up this section. There is the scene between Sharon and Jimmy Sr (pp. 152–4), that between Sharon and her friends (pp. 155–6), the third-person passage about Sharon and her book and her conversation with Jimmy Sr (pp. 156–60), another short passage about Sharon (p. 160), and the conversation between Jimmy Sr and Veronica and the arrival of Larrygogan (pp. 160–8).
— Consider the differences in these passages. In particular, look at the third-person passages that take us into Sharon's thoughts on pp. 156–7 and on p. 160. Work out the ways in which these differ from the dialogue sections. Ask yourself why it might be important that we know about what Sharon is feeling and thinking.

Focus on: character

DECIDE . . .
— How sympathetic are you to Sharon? What is making you feel that way? Shut the book and write down five key words

to describe her character. Where – in the text – have these ideas come from?

Focus on: language

ASK YOURSELF IF IT'S FUNNY? . . .

— On p. 157 Sharon asks Jimmy Sr, 'What's perception?' He says, 'Sweat . . . Why?' Is this funny? How does it relate to the way that Doyle uses language in the book as a whole?

Focus on: narrative structure

CONSIDER AND CONNECT . . .

— On p. 163 the twins arrive home with the puppy. Veronica says they can't keep it. Then she says they can. What is the point of this episode in relation to the themes and concerns of the novel as a whole?

SECTION 3
(pp. 168–75)

Focus on: the body

PUT TOGETHER . . .

— Look at the subject matter for each of the scenes in this section. Sharon bleeds, Larrygogan shits in the hall, Sharon is sick, Jimmy Sr complains about his sandwiches, Sharon examines her symptoms. How does each of these episodes connect to the others? Why might they all go in here, just at this particular point in the plot?

SECTION 4
(pp. 176–81)

Focus on: language

RELATE . . .

— The twins are discussing what mammies and daddies say to each other first thing in the morning. What has Jimmy Sr said to Veronica? How does this connect to the running joke about Veronica desperately trying to get her family not to use 'bad' language? How does that joke itself connect to the methods of Doyle's storytelling technique and to the themes of the novel as a whole?

SECTION 5
(pp. 181–6)

Focus on: the mystery

LOOK BACK AND CONSIDER . . .

— Sharon decides that she must tell her friends about her pregnancy tomorrow, but she's anxious about the fact that they'll ask her who the father is. Why do you suppose she doesn't want anyone to know? Have you guessed at who the father might be? Do you suppose it is someone we have already met in the novel?

— Now (pp. 184–6) we are told what happened when Sharon got pregnant. How much more information are you given here? How does this add to the mystery?

Focus on: Sharon and what happened to her

ASK YOURSELF . . .
— On p. 185 Sharon remembers – reluctantly – what happened. 'She'd wondered a few times if what had happened could be called rape. She didn't know.' What do you think?

Focus on: tragedy and comedy

DEFINE AND CATEGORISE . . .
— *The Snapper* is considered a comic novel. Look up the definition of comedy. When you get to the end you will be able to see clearly whether or not it fits that definition. At the same time – here at least – it is sad. Is it also tragic? Check out the literary definition of 'tragedy', then ask yourself the question again. If what happened to Sharon is not – strictly speaking – 'tragic', work out why it's not, and what it is.
— Finally, consider the way that Doyle moves from hilarious situations to very serious ones and back again. What does this mix of genres and scenes do to you as a reader?

Focus on: fathers

CONSIDER AND RELATE . . .
— Many of the older men in this story are fathers. Many of the younger ones are too – or are about to be. What does it mean to be a father? What does it suggest that Sharon cannot remember the opening of the Lord's Prayer (p. 168). Is it, in fact, the Lord's Prayer that she is failing to remember?
— Note down the different fathers that you meet in this novel and consider their own attitudes to fatherhood.

SECTION 6
(pp. 186–97)

Focus on: annunciation and revelation

COMPARE . . .

— Sharon tells the rest of her family about the baby. She tells her friends. Compare and contrast the two scenes. Then look back at Section 1 and compare what happened when Sharon told her father (and mother – just prior to the novel's opening).

Focus on: the mystery

REASSESS . . .

— In this section we find out who the father of Sharon's baby is. How? Why in this way? Look back over the novel to see what you already know about this man. How does this make you reassess all that has gone before? What do you think now about Sharon's predicament? And what do you think of him?

SECTION 7
(pp. 198–213)

Focus on: the change of focus

ANALYSE . . .

— At this point (p. 198) the scene slightly shifts and for the first time we are given a clear picture of Jimmy Sr and his drinking mates. Why now? How does this help to widen – and to narrow – the focus of the story?

Focus on: fathers

INTERPRET . . .

— On p. 212 there is a short – very short – scene between Sharon and her father. Why is it here? On p. 213 there is another short – very short – scene between Sharon and the twins. Consider how these two tiny episodes help construct your perception of Sharon's relation to her father.

SECTION 8
(pp. 213–21)

Focus on: identity

CONSIDER . . .

— Read the first few pages of this section and think about how each of these characters identifies themselves – who they are, what they do, why they matter: Darren, the twins, Sharon, the woman doctor Sharon sees. In what ways does this section contribute to the theme of the construction of identity in the novel as a whole?

Focus on: the mystery

QUESTION . . .

— How is the story of George Burgess's reaction to Sharon's pregnancy being expanded now? What do you make of his reactions and behaviour? Do you care about him? If not, why not? How are your reactions as a reader being manipulated by the structure and emphases of the text?

SECTION 9
(pp. 221–8)

Focus on: point of view

WEIGH UP . . .
— Consider the balance of the points of view in this confrontation between Sharon and Burgess. Whose side are you on? How do the techniques employed in the text manipulate your feelings?

Focus on: power and identity

PONDER AND NAME . . .
— Who has the power by the end of this scene? Why does it matter to Sharon? Why does it matter to you as a reader? Why do you want her to come away 'victorious'? Note the use of the word 'power'.
— Then look back to pp. 184–6 and the story of what happened to Sharon or what Sharon did – which was what? What name would you give to what happened then? A ride? Rape? Seduction? Fucking? Date rape? Being taken advantage of? Making love? Having sex? Impregnation? How does that scene in the car park connect to this one in Burgess's front room?

ASK YOURSELF . . .
— How has this episode changed a) your idea of who Sharon is, and b) Sharon's idea of who Sharon is?

SECTION 10
(pp. 228–43)

Focus on: humour

LOOK OVER AND DEFINE . . .
— Take any ONE of the short scenes in this passage and try to define the version of the humour, or the genre of the humour displayed there. It might help you to choose from this list: situation comedy, farce, slapstick, wordplay, toilet humour, puns.
— How often is it necessary for someone, or some group of people, to be the butt of the jokes? Does the fact that someone has to suffer, is put at a disadvantage, make it any less funny?

Focus on: romance or not?

TRANSFORM AND ASSESS . . .
— 'Was Mister Burgess getting all romantic on her? Sharon wondered. Jesus, that was disgusting. Maybe he's gone weird, like one of those men on the News——' (p. 243). So far we have only ever heard about Burgess from Sharon's point of view or that of her father. Think about him now and his actions now. Then, in no more than five hundred words, write the story of what happened and what is happening to him now from the point of view of Burgess. Does this change of focus change your attitude to him at all?

SECTION 11
(pp. 244–53)

Focus on: families and consequences

CONSIDER THE POINT OF VIEW . . .
— Think now about Doris Burgess. How does she react to

what she suspects? What do you think of her reaction? And of Jimmy Sr and Veronica's reaction to her reaction? And of Sharon's reaction to their reaction to Doris?

SECTION 12
(pp. 253–65)

Focus on: men and women, sex and romance

COMPARE AND CONNECT . . .
— Sharon invents the story about the Spanish sailor and Jackie says it's just like the film *Letter to Brezhnev* (p. 257). Look over the story that Sharon tells Jackie. It's a fantasy, but ask yourself how you know that it is a fantasy and where Sharon – given that she has never experienced anything like this – has got the constituents of this story from. Compare the fairy tale with the realities of the couples that you have met in this book so far – or in the earlier novel in the trilogy, *The Commitments*. Then connect this to the ballroom dancing that the twins are learning, and the sequinned dresses that Veronica is making. How do your own ideas on sex and romance, and on men's and women's attitudes to the same, connect to what is going on here?

Focus on: Jimmy Sr and Sharon

PONDER . . .
— In this section Jimmy Sr begins to feel differently about Sharon. Why is this, do you suppose?

SECTION 13
(pp. 265–74)

Focus on: character development

LOOK BACK AND COMPARE . . .

— Jimmy Rabbitte and Sharon meet on the stairs (pp. 270–2). If you have read *The Commitments*, where Jimmy was a major character, consider how this section enlarges on what you knew about him there. How is his character being developed? If you are planning to go on to read *The Van*, remember to keep a look out for more changes in Jimmy's life there. You might also like to look back and find the first time we met Sharon in *The Commitments* and compare that scene with this.

Focus on: language

ASK YOURSELF . . .

— Why, given the terms of the novel, and of the trilogy as a whole, is it significant that Jimmy has decided to take elocution lessons?

RESEARCH . . .

— The way people speak has always been used as an indicator of class or status. If you are interested in this issue, you might like to research it further and think about the implications of this social assumption. A useful and interesting book on the subject is Lynda Mugglestone's *Talking Proper: The Rise of Accent as Social Symbol* (1995).

SECTION 14
(pp. 274–81)

Focus on: fathers and daughters

REWRITE AND TRANSFORM . . .

— Sharon and Jimmy Sr's relationship deteriorates further. Work out how this breaks down across this section. What is the problem? Is it to do with social standing (among Jimmy's mates), guilt, responsibility, failure? How much of the problem is to do with the fact that Jimmy Sr and Sharon don't speak to each other honestly and fully about their feelings?

— Write a short account of this breakdown, first from Jimmy's point of view, and then from Sharon's point of view. How does this help to assess their behaviour towards one another?

SECTION 15
(pp. 281–94)

Focus on: Sharon, power and men and women

DECIDE . . .

— Sharon tackles the problem of her father (pp. 285–7). Why is it Sharon who makes this move? How does this confrontation connect to her earlier confrontation with Burgess (pp. 221–8)?

CONSIDER THESE STATEMENTS . . .

— Look at each of these statements. Which, in your opinion, are true and which false? How does thinking about these issues help to focus your reading of Doyle?

● Men are hopeless at talking about feelings.
● Men are all the same – they're only interested in food and sex.

- A woman, a dog and a walnut tree, the more you beat them, the better they be.
- Girls always talk everything over.
- Men discuss; women gossip.
- A woman's place is in the home.
- A whistling woman and a crowing hen are neither good for God nor men.
- Silence is a woman's best garment.

SECTION 16
(pp. 294–309)

Focus on: the family

CONSIDER . . .

— Matters are mended between Sharon and Jimmy Sr. How does this resolution affect the rest of the family? How much is said in words? How much is conveyed by actions? And which actions? Why is it important that Jimmy makes the joke about the gnome being the 'spit o' George Burgess' (p. 309)?

SECTION 17
(pp. 310–19)

Focus on: language and clichés

RESEARCH . . .

— Look over this section and jot down all the clichés you can find. Examples might include 'lady of leisure' and 'like the cavalry'. When you have your list, find out the origins of the expressions. Ask yourself what a cliché is and how it works. How much does it rely upon shared knowledge?

SECTION 18
(pp. 319–28)

Focus on: Jimmy Sr

ASSESS . . .

— Jimmy Sr has been reading a book about women. He has taken over the running of the cycling club. Now he is mowing the lawn. Why? What do you think of his offer to be with Sharon at the birth (p. 328)? Assess the ways in which Jimmy Sr might be changing.

SECTION 19
(pp. 328–38)

Focus on: narrative structure

ANALYSE THE SHAPE . . .

— All the threads of the story are coming together in this section. Sharon gets drunk with Jackie. Jimmy Sr makes tea. The twins come back from their dancing competition. Jimmy Jr is on the radio. And . . . Sharon starts going into labour. How has Doyle shaped this climactic section? And in what ways are the reactions of the reader and our attitudes to the characters being manipulated?

Focus on: humour

FIND . . .

— Look for examples of the kind of humour that this text has employed throughout. 'Look at her condition,' says Jackie, and a man at the bar replies, 'She doesn't look tha' bad' (p. 328). Jimmy drives Sharon in labour and on p. 338 says, 'Good girl. It's only the oul' cervix dilatin'. ——It could happen to a

75

bishop, wha'.' Why are these examples – and the other ones you've found – funny? Think about the way they work. Here is a list to help you: exaggeration, contradiction, punning, wordplay, understatement, overstatement, (deliberate) misunderstanding, inappropriateness.

SECTION 20
(pp. 338–40)

Focus on: endings

RESEARCH AND COMPARE . . .
— A baby is born. Look for other novels that end with a birth or with the promise of a birth, and compare them with this ending. Examples might include: George Eliot's *Middlemarch*, Charles Dickens's *Great Expectations* (1860–1), Ian McEwan's *The Child in Time* (1987), A. S. Byatt's *A Whistling Woman* (2003), Sebastian Faulkes's *Birdsong* (1994).

ASK YOURSELF . . .
— Why does Sharon call the baby Georgina? Why is she laughing? Is this an ending?

Looking over the whole novel

QUESTIONS FOR DISCUSSION OR ESSAYS
1. Is Sharon the heroine of *The Snapper*, or is Jimmy Sr the hero?

2. 'A novel about the triumphs and indignities of family life.' Do you agree with this summary?

3. Would you describe *The Snapper* as a chauvinist novel?

4. Analyse the mix of tragedy and comedy in *The Snapper*.

5. 'Words, dialogue and voice are Roddy Doyle's greatest strengths.' Assess the justice of this comment in the light of your reading of *The Snapper*.

6. 'Roddy Doyle's preoccupations are with the margins: marginal characters, marginal settings, marginal to history. But this is where real life is lived.' Discuss.

7. How far is the Barrytown setting essential to the structure and themes of *The Barrytown Trilogy*?

8. Analyse the development of any TWO of these characters from *The Barrytown Trilogy*: Sharon, Jimmy Rabbitte, Jimmy Sr, Leslie, Bimbo.

Reading guides for

THE VAN

BEFORE YOU BEGIN TO READ . . .
— Read the interview with Doyle. You will see there that he identifies a number of themes and techniques in this novel:

- Identity and sense of place
- Class
- Dialogue

Other themes that may be useful to consider while reading the novel include:

- Food
- Comedy
- Employment – or otherwise – and pride
- Friendship
- Men and women

Reading activities: detailed analysis

Focus on: the title

EXPLORE THE CONNOTATIONS . . .

— If you haven't read this novel yet (if you have, then this question is not for you), what do you think it is going to be about, given that all you know is the name of the author and the title?

— If you haven't read this novel, but you have read *The Commitments* or *The Snapper*, what does the title suggest to you that you will be reading about? Ask yourself the question again when you have read to the end of the novel.

Focus on: the dedication

ASK YOURSELF . . .

— What is funny – both funny peculiar and funny ha ha – about this dedication, and what makes it different from the usual kinds of dedication? When you've got to the end of the book, look again and ask yourself why the dedication is appropriate.

SECTION I
(pp. 347–56)

Focus on: beginnings and introductions

WEIGH UP . . .

— At the beginning of this novel we are introduced, or rein-troduced, to a number of characters that we have already met in *The Commitments* and *The Snapper*. Think about how they have changed. How much further on in time are we from when we last met these characters? And how do you know?

— How does Doyle re-establish the scene and our connections and interest in these characters? How would you categorise the tone of the opening scenes: tragic, light-hearted, warm, funny, sad, contented? And how would you describe the feelings of the family for each other?

SECTION 2
(pp. 356–92)

Focus on: more changes and characterisation

SEEK OUT AND INTERPRET . . .

— Jimmy Sr goes to the library (p. 357); Jimmy Jr is living in Clontarf with his girlfriend Aoife (p. 359); Veronica is doing night classes (p. 361). What does each of these new facts contribute to the development of these characters? Look for other examples of change. There is Jimmy Sr's drinking, for instance (p. 357). And what about Leslie? He is mentioned on p. 359. What has happened to him? How does that square with what you knew of him from *The Snapper*?

Focus on: allusions to time and place

LIST AND ASSESS . . .

— Look over this section and note down all the allusions to real people, places, books, and circumstances that you can find. These might include Arsenal (p. 363), 'HERE WE GO' (p. 365), Kylie (p. 370), *The Magic Roundabout* and *Postman Pat* (p. 372), Bob Geldof (p. 375), 'Big Fun' and 'Wet Wet Wet' (p. 390). What do you know about any or all of these? Are there things in this list that have already dated? Remember that *The Van* was published in 1991. Imagine that you were reading this novel in ten years' time. How much of this would a new reader recognise? Does it matter whether or not a reader recognises these allusions? How much would you be able to guess at from the context and information given to you in the text?

AND CONSIDER . . .

— Veronica is reading William Golding's *Lord of the Flies* (1954) (p. 371). Jimmy Sr decides to read Alexandre Dumas's *The Man in the Iron Mask* (1846) (p. 362). What do you know about either or both of these novels? Why do you suppose that they have chosen these books to read? How relevant is either book to the lives of Veronica and Jimmy? References to texts inside texts are (almost) never accidental. As a judicious reader, you are entitled to make assumptions about the relevance of the allusion. For instance: in Choderlos de Laclos's novel *Les Liaisons Dangereuses* (1782), the rakish Valmont has made a bet that he can seduce La Presidente de Tourvel, a woman well known for her fidelity to her husband and for her piety. He does not seem to be getting very far, but he bribes her maid to find out what books she is reading in bed. It turns out that one of them is an early English novel by Samuel Richardson called *Clarissa* (1748–9). This particular novel tells the story – at length, and with much erotic detail – of the heroine, Clarissa

Harlowe, who is attracted to, pursued by and eventually raped by the wicked anti-hero Lovelace. When he finds this out, Valmont is pleased and encouraged. But both in his case, and in the case of we readers, the allusion depends on our knowledge of the text mentioned. If you do know either or both *The Man in the Iron Mask* or *Lord of the Flies*, consider how these references and allusions might help to make a subtle parallel or give some kind of message about what is going on in the text of *The Van*.

Focus on: language

NOTE AND ASK YOURSELF . . .

— In all three of the novels that make up *The Barrytown Trilogy*, there is a distinctive use of certain kinds of slang or dialect or local idioms that colours the speech of the characters. Look over this section and find as many specific words as you can – such as 'brasser', 'codding', 'manky', 'eejit', 'telly', 'bejesus' and 'eccers'. How many of these words would you use? How many would your friends use? Does it depend on who you are and where you live? If you don't immediately understand a word, does it matter?

COMPARE . . .

— If you have read Alice Walker's *The Color Purple* (1983), you will know that Celie and the other characters in that novel use a slang or an idiom that is designed to represent their dialogue. Compare the use of idiomatic language in Walker's novel with that used by Doyle in the trilogy. In what ways does the use of such language create a sense of authenticity and spontaneity even if the effect is, in fact, carefully manipulated?

SECTION 3
(pp. 392–411)

Focus on: waiting

ADD UP . . .

— Jimmy Sr is unemployed and has been so for some time. On p. 395 we are told that he had 'this feeling in his guts all the time . . . It was bad, a bad sort of excitement, and he couldn't get rid of it'. What do you suppose this suggests? What are the other effects of the fact that Jimmy does not have any work? Look over this section and note down the ways in which Doyle builds the idea of this absence out of the things that are affected by it. Here is a list to help you: lack of money, self-esteem, loneliness, boredom, not being able to give, too much time unused, impatience, lack of stories to tell and share.

Focus on: allusions

RESEARCH AND COMPARE . . .

— Jimmy Sr gives up on *The Man in the Iron Mask* (1846) and starts reading Charles Dickens's *David Copperfield* (1849–50) (p. 396). He particularly likes and is intrigued by the character in that novel called Micawber. Find out about that part of the story (chapter XVII is one place to start). Why might Jimmy be so interested in Micawber? What does this tell you about Jimmy?

Focus on: representations of Christmas

RESEARCH AND COMPARE . . .

— On pp. 398–408 we are given the story of the Rabbitte family's Christmas Day. Find other books which include a Christmas scene. There is, of course, a famous scene in Charles Dickens's *A Christmas Carol* (1843), but there is also one near the beginning of his *Great Expectations* (1860–1, chapter 4). Louisa May Alcott's *Little Women* (1868) also begins with a famous scene set on Christmas Day.

— Jot down the associations that go with the idea of Christmas. Begin with spiritual and religious connections and then go on to social, familial and commercial associations. When you have your list, consider why Christmas is so often the background setting to important moments in fiction. Then compare the scene played out by Jimmy Sr and Veronica and the rest with the other fictional Christmas scene that you have found. In what ways are the concerns the same? In what ways are they different?

Focus on: history on the margins

RESEARCH AND THINK . . .
— On p. 410 Jimmy goes to the library and reads the papers. He also watches the television and thinks about what is happening in the world and, especially, with the 'Warsaw Pact' countries. Three world leaders are also mentioned: Margaret Thatcher, George Bush and Mikhail Gorbachev. What do you know about these leaders? What do you know about what was going on, politically, at the time? How might those events be reflected in the things that are happening to the Rabbitte family?

RESEARCH AND COMPARE . . .
— Ian McEwan's novel *Black Dogs* (1992) is set around this same time, but the events that Doyle merely glances at here figure more prominently in McEwan's novel. Compare the uses that the two writers make of recent history.

SECTION 4
(pp. 411–25)

Focus on: Bimbo

LOOK BACK AND COMPARE . . .

— Bimbo tells Jimmy that he's been made redundant. Look back over *The Snapper* and consider how Bimbo's character has been developed so far. What new elements can you add to your image of his character, going on the information given to you in this section? What specific details from the text help you to place him and picture him? Point to phrases, key images and jot down the page numbers. This will all be useful later on.

Focus on: men and women and power

ANALYSE . . .

— Bimbo, Bertie and Jimmy go from a discussion about Bimbo's redundancy to a conversation about women and sex. Why is this? What possible connection can there be? Jimmy feels slightly anxious about the tone of the conversation. Why do you think this might be? What do you think of Bertie's story about how he bought a packet of crisps – that he hates – just to get Mandy to bend over to pick them out of the box (p. 416)?

LOOK BACK . . .

— In the light of this episode, look back at the passage in *The Snapper* where Jimmy hears that Burgess had been boasting that Sharon was 'a ride' (p. 216–8). Consider what connections you can make between these two episodes.

Focus on: jokes

ASSESS THE EFFECTS . . .

— Look over this section for examples of the kinds of jokes that the gang of boys make. For instance, where Bertie tells how his wife Vera had been asked to help clean the church and he says, 'She doesn't even help to dirty the fuckin' place on Sunday mornin's' (p. 415), or the moment on p. 419 where Jimmy Sr says, 'She's a daisy,' and Paddy quips, 'An' you're a tulip.' How do these jokes work? On what givens or skills in the audience do they rely? Why are they funny? Do they work through: exaggeration, overstatement, understatement, word-play, association of images, puns, inappropriate connections?

SECTION 5
(pp. 426–46)

Focus on: time and change

LOOK OVER AND CONNECT . . .

— Look at the opening sentences of each small section here: 'The next couple of weeks were great' (p. 426); 'There were bad times as well, of course' (p. 434); 'Jimmy Jr came around with four cans of Carlsberg' (p. 437); 'What're her parents like?' (p. 439); 'He washed his face' (p. 442). Most of these are to do with Jimmy Sr and Bimbo. But one is about Jimmy Jr and what is happening in his life. Can you make a connection or an opposition between these scenes? How does the family scene and the discussion about Aoife's parents illuminate or counter-point what is going on with Jimmy Sr?

SECTION 6
(pp. 446–62)

Focus on: the van

THINK ABOUT THE SETTING UP . . .
— How has Bimbo's idea about getting a chipper van been set up so far in the novel? Two episodes in particular help to frame Bimbo's decision: the moment when Jimmy found him applying for a job in McDonald's, and the moment when the lads came out of the pub to find that the old chipper van was not in its usual spot. Look back over those episodes and see how they set up and anticipate Bimbo's new resolution.

Focus on: men and women, sex and power

CONSIDER . . .
— Jimmy Sr and Bimbo watch the three girls going by (pp. 447–9). Remember the conversation about Mandy and about sex in the pub on the night when Bimbo told Jimmy and Bertie about being made redundant. Why might it be that this scene with the three young girls takes place just around the time when Bimbo's van is about to appear on the scene? What is the connection?

Focus on: partnership

NOTE . . .
— Bimbo asks Jimmy Sr to become his partner in the van (pp. 461–2). Note this moment. Why might it be important? Ask yourself the question again when you have finished reading the novel.

AND COMPARE . . .
— How might this moment between Bimbo and Jimmy Sr

be connected to events that took place in either or both *The Commitments* and *The Snapper*?

SECTION 7
(pp. 462–79)

Focus on: Jimmy Sr and Veronica, Jimmy and Bimbo, Bimbo and Maggie

COMPARE AND CONTRAST . . .

— Think about the three main relationships described in this section. How are Jimmy Sr and Veronica getting on? In what ways has their relationship been strengthened by the van project? And what about Bimbo and his wife Maggie? Meanwhile, what is happening to the friendship between the two men? What is the significance of Sharon's request to work in the van and Jimmy Sr's casual agreement (p. 466)?

SECTION 8
(pp. 479–504)

Focus on: the first time

COMPARE AND DETERMINE . . .

— Jimmy Sr and Bimbo are preparing for the night when they will take the van out for the first time. They practise making batter; they cut up the potatoes for the chips; they add the burger sign; and they pack the van. But there are two preludes to their serving of their first burger: the van nearly crashes, sending water and other equipment over the floor (pp. 485–6; and they go into the Hikers to watch the Ireland v. England match (pp. 486–90). How do all these episodes build the tension as the grand opening of the burger van looms? How would you characterise the different elements in terms of triumph and tragedy? In what ways are your reactions being manipulated by the build-up? How does this technique create and continue a narrative drive?

Focus on: contradictions

ASSESS THE EFFECT . . .

> Jimmy Sr was bursting; not for a piss, with love. He hugged Bimbo. He hugged Bertie. He hugged Paddy. He even hugged Larry O'Rourke. He loved everyone. There was Sharon. He got over to her and hugged her, and then all her friends . . .
>
> Everyone in the place sang. Jimmy Sr hated the song, but it didn't matter . . .
>
> —It's a great song, isn't it? said Bimbo.
> —Ah, yeah, said Jimmy Sr.
> It was that sort of day (pp. 489–90).

— How important do you think these contradictions are? What tensions may still lie, unresolved, beneath the cheerful surface of unity and consent?

ANALYSE THE TONE . . .

— By the end of the evening Jimmy Sr, Sharon and Bimbo have all suffered; they are exhausted, they are messy and covered in fat, Sharon's shoes are ruined, they have made a lot of money. Jimmy proposes a toast with a greasy can of warm drink (pp. 503–4). How would you define the tone of this scene? Consider which of the following terms is most appropriate (some of them may not be appropriate at all): farce, bathos, pathos, triumph, slapstick, situation comedy, tragedy.

NOTE . . .

— 'At the end of the week – next Friday – he was going to put money on the table in front of Veronica, and say nothing' (p. 504). Why is this important?

SECTION 9
(pp. 504–33)

Focus on: continuation and consolidation

MAKE A LIST . . .

— Look over this section and make a list of the scenes and events described here. Begin with the scene on pp. 504–5 where Sharon and Jimmy Sr realise how they have been burned by the splattering of hot fat.

— When you have your list, consider how this is building the story of *The Van* and its progress.

Focus on: language

CONSIDER . . .

— A boy gives his order for sausage and a large portion of chips but turns it into 'A large an' a dunphy' (p. 506). Do you know what a 'dunphy' is? If not, can you guess from the context?

— In what ways does this show how the characters in Barrytown invent language – and change language? If you look at the interview with Doyle you will see that he has something to say about this (pp. 16–18).

— How does this play with, and interest, in language work out in the novel as a whole?

Focus on: dispute and confrontation

WORK OUT . . .

— Darren and Jimmy Sr quarrel about the fact that Darren is vegetarian and Jimmy is less than particular about mixing meat and fish – and everything else. Think about this confrontation – which is, more or less, resolved on p. 533. Remember it later in relation to what happens between Jimmy Sr and Bimbo.

SECTION 10
(pp. 534–58)

Focus on: the nappy episode

DECIDE . . .

— What do you think is the point of this long scene? How does it connect back to issues you might already have thought about? How might it look forward and suggest what is coming up?

Focus on: allegiances

ASSESS . . .

— 'Bimbo and Maggie were the ones in charge' (p. 554). Do you agree? What does it matter? How might Jimmy have been more 'in charge'?

SECTION 11
(pp. 558–601)

Focus on: the break-up

TRACE . . .

— Look over this section and work out the several stages in the disintegration of Bimbo and Jimmy Sr's relationship. How does this happen? Should it have happened? What could Jimmy have done differently? And should he?

LIST AND INTERPRET . . .

— Jimmy and Bimbo go out on the town. If you look you will see that several unusual words are introduced in this section for the first time. Look out for them and list them. Why do they appear now? What might they suggest about the deterioration of Jimmy and Bimbo's friendship?

ASSESS . . .

— Jimmy can't remember Bimbo's real name (p. 590). Think about this and judge what it implies.

SECTION 12
(pp. 603–33)

Focus on: men and women

LOOK OVER . . .

— Think about the relations between Maggie and Bimbo and between Jimmy and Veronica in this section. Look also at the way in which the narrative describes Bimbo and Jimmy as if they were a married couple. What does this suggest about the relationship between friends, and between husbands and wives?

Focus on: endings

DECIDE . . .
— How many endings does *The Van* have? Could the novel have ended in some other place? There is the ending as the van itself is pushed into the water. (But can it be rescued? Will it be?) And there is the ending between Veronica and Jimmy. Is this an ending? Or a beginning?

Looking over the whole novel

QUESTIONS FOR DISCUSSION OR ESSAYS
1. '*The Van* is a love story.' Discuss.

2. Consider the use of dialogue in *The Van*.

3. Analyse the running theme of the use of 'bad language' in *The Van*.

4. Consider the role played by Sharon, Veronica, Darren or Leslie in *The Van*.

5. 'Maggie and Veronica are the real heroines of *The Van*.' Do you agree?

Contexts, comparisons and complementary readings

THE BARRYTOWN TRILOGY

These sections suggest contextual and comparative ways of reading these works by Doyle. You can put your reading in a social, historical or literary context. You can make comparisons – again, social, literary or historical – with other texts or art works. Or you can choose complementary works (of whatever kind) – that is, art works, literary works, social reportage or facts which in some way illuminate the text by sidelights or interventions which you can make into a telling framework. Some of the suggested contexts are directly connected to the book, in that they will give you precise literary or social frames in which to situate the novel. In turn, these are either related to the period within which the novel is set, or to the time – now – when you are reading it. Some of these examples are designed to suggest books or other texts that may make useful sources for comparison (or for complementary purposes) when you are reading one or more of the books in *The Barrytown Trilogy*. Again, they may be related to literary or critical themes, or they may be relevant to social and cultural themes current 'then' or 'now'.

Focus on: the idea of a trilogy and the number 3

CONSIDER STRUCTURE . . .

— What is a trilogy? What is the cultural significance of the number 3? When you have read all three books in what is now called *The Barrytown Trilogy*, think about the relation of each individual book to the other two. Would it make any difference if you thought that Doyle had planned out three books before he began writing? Do you suppose, from your own reading of the text, that he did?

THINK ABOUT THE TEXTS . . .

— How many examples of threes exist in the texts themselves? If you divide the characters into groups of three what patterns do you come up with? Who complicates threes?

THINK ABOUT CULTURE . . .

— Where else is the idea of 'three' important? For example, in Christianity what is the Holy Trinity? Heaven, Earth and Hell, as well as Heaven, Purgatory and Hell, form fundamental 'threes'.

— How do these significant meanings influence your reading of the text? For example, you may have focused on the relation of three to Christianity and the Holy Trinity: God the Father, God the Son and God the Holy Spirit. How do you interpret these roles in relation to *The Commitments*, *The Snapper* and *The Van*?

DISCUSS . . .

— Discuss the differing meanings for three that seem significant to you. Is three important for other reasons? Why do you suppose it is so often used in fairy tales, such as, for instance, *Goldilocks and the Three Bears*? Why might it be significant that things often happen three times in fairy tales? Or that there are often three sisters – or three brothers, or three things to choose from? How is its meaning different here and what does that suggest to you about Doyle's narrative?

THE COMMITMENTS

Focus on: parents

COMPARE AND ASSESS . . .
— In 2002, Doyle published the story of his parents in *Rory and Ita*. The dedication of his first novel *The Commitments* was to his parents. How do these facts square with the treatment of the theme of parents and children in the novels overall?

Focus on: comedy

RESEARCH AND COMPARE . . .
— Find out about other novels that are presented as 'comic', and particularly look for those that are mainly set as dialogue or as interconnected episodes or scenes. A good example to choose would be Joseph Heller's *Catch-22* (1961). Others might include Charles Dickens's *The Pickwick Papers* (1837), Samuel Beckett's *Murphy* (1938), Flann O'Brien's *The Third Policeman* (1967) or Jeanette Winterson's *Oranges Are Not the Only Fruit* (1985).

Focus on: Irish comedy

RESEARCH . . .
— A useful introduction to this specific area of study might be *The Penguin Book of Irish Comic Writing*, edited by Ferdia MacAnna (1996). This selection includes the story 'Vincent' by Roddy Doyle, as well as stories by Samuel Beckett, James Joyce, Molly Keene, Bernard MacLaverty, Spike Milligan, Mary Morissey, Flann O'Brien, Bridget O'Connor, Sean O'Faolain and Moya Roddy.

Focus on: pop songs

RESEARCH AND COMPARE . . .
— *The Commitments* is a novel based on the premise of a counterpoint to the story provided by the songs the band sings. This is a common technique in films where soundtracks provide the tone and the period feel of the setting. Examples of such use of songs in film might include Sam Mendes's *American Beauty* (1999) or Hal Ashby's *Coming Home* (1978). Books that use this technique are more unusual but include Nick Hornby's *High Fidelity* (1995) and, more recently, his *Thirty One Songs* (2003). Look out for any such example of the exploitation of popular songs and compare the method to that used in *The Commitments*.

Focus on: class, race and liberation

RESEARCH AND COMPARE . . .
— On p. 13 Jimmy makes his important speech about class exclusion and compares the Irish, and Dubliners, with the

exploitation of 'niggers'. If you have read Roddy Doyle's later novel *A Star Called Henry* (1999), you will remember that Henry Smart's Granny Nash is keen on reading – and especially on reading books by women. During the course of his travels he provides her with a number of books with titles like *Behind the Scenes: or, Thirty Years a Slave and Four Years in the White House*, or *The Wonderful Adventures of Mrs Seacole in Many Lands*, or *The History of Mary Prince, a West Indian Slave, Related by Herself*. If you know about any of these books, then ask yourself why and how it is relevant that while Henry is fighting for Irish independence, Granny Nash is surviving on a diet of such books. If you don't know any of these books, can you guess what their subjects might be? Find out, if not. Then ask yourself the same question.

— Finally, consider how this strand in *A Star Called Henry* might relate to Jimmy's speech in the earlier *The Commitments*.

THE SNAPPER

Focus on: unmarried mothers

COMPARE AND ASSESS . . .

— Find other books that deal with the story of a woman having a baby out of wedlock. In particular, look for books from different periods of history and consider the different ways in which such girls are treated. Here is a list of suggestions: Mary Wollstonecraft's *Mary, or The Wrongs of Woman* (1788), Nathaniel Hawthorne's *The Scarlet Letter* (1850), Elizabeth Gaskell's *Ruth* (1853), Elizabeth Barrett Browning's *Aurora Leigh* (1857), George Eliot's *Adam Bede* (1859), Thomas Hardy's *Tess of the d'Urbervilles* (1891), Lynne Reid Banks's *The L-shaped Room* (1960), Margaret Drabble's *The Millstone* (1966), Alice Walker's *The Color Purple* (1983).

— Think particularly about the circumstances in which each character becomes pregnant. Was it as a result of seduction, rape, choice, foolishness, ignorance?

— How does that character's family react? – are they supportive, angry, rejecting, sympathetic?

— How do the differing societies depicted react? – are they condemning, critical, careless, helpful, understanding?

— How much does the woman who has the baby suffer? And in what ways? Does she keep the baby? If not, why not? What happens to the baby, and how will the facts of his or her circumstances at birth affect their future life?

— How important is it to anyone in these novels to know the name of the father? What happens to the father? Does he suffer? If so, in what ways?

— How does this work help you to understand the ways in which society and social attitudes change? (And don't assume that change will always be for the better.)

Focus on: men and women

RESEARCH AMONG YOUR FRIENDS . . .

— Thinking about the events discussed in *The Snapper*, ask around your friends about their ideas on relations between men and women and, in particular, how they think men and women talk to each other, what they expect from each other, whether or not they believe that men and women can be friends (without a sexual context).

LIST AND ANALYSE VOCABULARY USED IN RELATION TO GENDER . . .

— Compile two lists, one for traits that you consider to be typical of men, the other for traits that you think are typical of women. Where would you put such traits as: competitive, co-operative, conformist, creative, liking hierarchy and power, having a sense of justice, liking to organise others, submissive, liking machines, sincere, intuitive, emotionally aware, caring, altruistic, sensitive, respecting authority, emotional, open to change?

— Once you've made these lists, consider whether there are any hard facts that will support or refute these attributions; if there are, seek out some of those facts to test your thesis. Alternatively, use these lists as a starting point for a discussion (with yourself or others) about men's and women's attitudes to shared issues such as sex, family, parenting, hierarchy, friendship and work.

SEARCH AND ANALYSE . . .

— Read John Gray's best-selling advice book *Men Are From Mars, Women Are From Venus: A Practical Guide for Improving Communication and Getting What You Want in Your Relationships* (1992), or else try Allan and Barbara Pease, *Why Men Don't Listen and Women Can't Read Maps: How we're different and what to do about it* (2001).

— More seriously, you might like to look at the some of the important books published recently on language and the differing ways in which men and women talk, such as Deborah Cameron, *The Feminist Critique of Language* (1990), or Deborah Tannen, ed., *Gender and Conversational Interaction* (1993).

— Consider your attitudes to the opposite sex in the light of these readings. Try to be honest, and write down what you really believe to be the good qualities (and also the bad) of your own sex. Now examine again the attitudes to relations between men and women in *The Snapper*. Do you agree with the assumptions and patterns set out there, or not? If not, why not?

ANALYSE AND INTERPRET . . .
— Proverbs and sayings – like jokes – can be revealing of a culture's shared attitudes. What does each of these proverbs below suggest about Western attitudes to relationships between men and women? Look for places in *The Snapper* where characters make similar sweeping statements about men and women and their relations. What purpose do those remarks serve a) in creating the characterisation of the person who speaks them, and b) in relation to the working out of this theme through the whole story?

- Never choose your women or your linen by candlelight.
- A woman and ship ever want mending.
- The hand that rocks the cradle rules the world.
- The female of the species is more deadly than the male.
- A woman's work is never done.
- Hell hath no fury like a woman scorned.
- He that will thrive must first ask his wife.
- A blind man's wife needs no paint.
- A young man married is a young man marred.
- A deaf husband and a blind wife are a happy couple.
- The husband is always the last to know.

THE VAN

Focus on: food and class

LOOK AROUND IN THE SUPERMARKET . . .
— You are in the supermarket and take to inspecting other

people's trolleys and baskets as they come to the checkout. How far do you judge a person by what they are eating – or buying? Is a person what they eat? What kind of person will have which of the following items in their basket?

- sliced white bread
- lard
- aromatic flavoured vinegar
- olive oil
- Tesco's Finest pork and apple sausages
- six-pack frozen pizza
- oven chips
- globe artichokes
- organic potatoes
- free-range eggs
- Coca-Cola
- own-brand chocolate biscuits
- family pack of Twix
- tinned tuna
- tuna in a jar in olive oil
- Perrier
- Stella

— What does this tell you about your own class assumptions?
— How does this relate to the food theme of *The Van* (and *The Snapper*)?

THINK ABOUT CHANGES ACROSS TIME . . .
Here is a list of foodstuffs. What kind of person would be eating which foods a) now, b) in the 1840s, and c) in the early 1700s?

- oysters
- mussels
- rabbit

- white bread
- black rye bread
- mashed potatoes

- venison
- tea
- coffee

- chicken
- pheasant
- chips
- truffles
- sugar
- fresh fish

THINK AGAIN ABOUT CHANGES ACROSS TIME . . .
— You have before you four persons:

- A: A twenty-five-year-old peasant living near a river in a fertile area of Kent, with his own plot of land, in the early fifteenth century. He has a clever wife who was taught to cook by her own mother.
- B: A fifty-year-old dowager, mother of the Duke of Norfolk, living at court in the early fifteenth century. She has always had servants.
- C: A forty-five-year-old, out-of-work lorry driver, living in the early twenty-first century in rented accommodation in Wales with his (not very provident) wife and three teenage children.
- D: A twenty-nine-year-old (ex?) pop star living now in a mansion in the country and a villa in the South of France with her star footballer husband and two young children.

Now ask yourself these questions and rank the four persons as indicated:

1. Who eats more – in terms of amounts of food or calories consumed?

2. Who eats with what? Knife and fork, chopsticks, fingers?

3. Who eats sugar?

4. Who eats the freshest food?

5. Who thinks about the preparation of food most?

6. Who eats at what time of day?

7. Who eats most meat?

8. Who eats food that has been organically produced?

9. Whose diet is likely to be most varied and balanced, i.e. with a small amount of protein (meat, fish, eggs), a moderate amount of carbohydrate (potatoes, bread, pasta), plenty of fresh fruit and vegetables, and very little fat or sugar?

10. Who gives the most amount of time to thinking about what they are eating?

Focus on: male bonding

RESEARCH AND CONSIDER . . .

— By the end of the novel Bimbo and Jimmy Sr are arguing: but this is not between mates, it is as if they are a married couple. Look over those passages. Then think about the ways in which men – in all-men situations – relate to each other. Find a text that is about this issue. This might be anything from the films *The Full Monty* (1997) or *Brassed Off* (1997) or *Gallipoli* (1981) or *Stand By Me* (1986), to the novel *Strange Meeting* (1971) by Susan Hill or even Shakespeare's play *Othello* (c. 1604) where Desdemona, Emilia and Bianca are the only women in the army garrison setting.

— Then ask yourself how much of this relation is about friendship and how much of it is about love – and what kinds of love. On this subject, you might like to read Eve Kosofsky Sedgewick's book *Between Men: English Literature and Male Homosocial Desire* (1985).

Paddy Clarke Ha Ha Ha

IN CLOSE-UP

Reading guides for

PADDY CLARKE HA HA HA

BEFORE YOU BEGIN TO READ . . .
— Read the interview with Doyle. You will see there that he identifies a number of themes and techniques in this novel:

- Dialogue
- The child's eye view
- Structure and method
- The setting

Other themes that may be useful to consider while reading the novel include:

- Comedy
- Reading
- First-person narrative
- Childhood cruelty
- The Family
- Innocence and experience

Reading activities: detailed analysis

Focus on: the title

CONSIDER THE EXPECTATIONS SET UP BY THE TITLE . . .
— The title points to the centrality of the ten-year-old narrator, Paddy Clarke, through whose eyes the events will be told. It also foregrounds the novel's themes of humour and cruelty, since it is a near-quotation of a chant on p. 281 in which some other children cruelly mock Paddy Clarke for his misfortune after his parents have separated. Consider the expectations the title sets up for the stylistic register of the novel, which is written in the vernacular of colloquial speech, with a vibrant mixture of slang, dialect and vulgarisms.

Focus on: the novel's structure

LOOK OVER . . .
— Flick through the novel to get an impression of its structure, which marked a departure for Doyle from the long sections of dialogue that characterised *The Barrytown Trilogy*. This novel is narrated by a ten-year-old boy, and the narrative sets out to represent how a child's mind works. In *Paddy Clarke Ha Ha Ha* there are no formal parts, chapter divisions or titles: the narrative is presented as vignettes that are run together, with

short gaps. Doyle has said that in *Paddy Clarke Ha Ha Ha* he set out to convey the amorphous fluidity of a child's conscious experience: the way a child's mind jumps around, connecting disparate ideas in surprising ways and creating a sort of continuity at a subconscious level. The narrative is ordered much in the manner of 'stream of consciousness', so that the links are sometimes obvious and sometimes not. Paddy makes sequential rather than consequential connections, often equating major issues with minor ones, without the discriminating judgement of an adult mind, but without an adult's predictability too. Doyle wrote the novel in episodes which he then rearranged and knitted together, a process he has compared to editing a film. As is often the case with Doyle, what may at first appear simple and artless is actually a considered effect – a literary decision made for specific ends.

Focus on: the setting

CONTEXTUALISE . . .

— *Paddy Clarke Ha Ha Ha* is set in the late 1960s in a fictional suburb of Dublin, Ireland, the same Barrytown suburb in which Doyle set his earlier novels *The Commitments*, *The Snapper* and *The Van* (*The Barrytown Trilogy*). In this trilogy, the residents of Barrytown are portrayed as an insular bunch, concerned entirely with their own immediate environment and indifferent to the wider issues of Irish history, politics or religion. Doyle records in *Rory and Ita* (2002), his memoir about his parents, that when his father came to Dublin he found it was 'like being in a different country. The philosophy was anti-Republican, anti-Gaelic, almost anti-Irish.' There is almost no mention in Doyle's early novels of the conflict in Northern Ireland, of the IRA, or of the Ulster Volunteer Force; and other issues of importance to the rest of Ireland, such as the European Union and financial scandals, hardly figure in the lives of his characters.

Doyle's characters inhabit the grey area between the working classes and the middle classes. Some are poor and uneducated; many are also unemployed. The elements that help them to survive lives that are grim and offer little hope for change are found in the network provided by community, friends and especially family, which is why Paddy Clarke finds the break-up of his family unit and of his group of friends so unsettling. If you want to gain a fuller picture of Barrytown, read any one of *The Barrytown Trilogy*.

SECTION I
(pp. 1–4)

Focus on: the opening

LISTEN TO THE RHYTHMS . . .

— Doyle portrays his characters more through how they speak than through descriptions of what they look like or how they act, and there is a subtle kind of music in Doyle's novels in the rhythms of the characters' speech. As you read these opening pages, pay attention to the rhythms of the prose, and especially to the rhythms of the dialogue.

Focus on: the child narrator

READ CLOSELY AND COMMENT . . .

— *Paddy Clarke Ha Ha Ha* marks a stylistic departure for Doyle in his use of a first-person narrator. The entire novel is told in the voice of a ten-year-old boy, so that Paddy Clarke's life, his relationships with his friends and family, and his innocent, open, jubilant views of the world are realised in great detail. He is quite an articulate boy for his age, but his views are those of a ten-year-old boy. Read the first four pages and consider how Paddy Clarke's voice, his idiom, his attitudes and his frames of reference reveal his character. How convincingly has Doyle entered the mind of a child in these opening pages, in your opinion? And in what ways are the episodes in these opening pages typical of childhood?

SECTION 2
(pp. 4–8)

Focus on: innocence and experience

NOTE THE LAYERS . . .

— Into the picture of the rumbustious but essentially innocent games of childhood, Doyle introduces some dissonant notes which the reader may spot but Paddy (as yet) does not. The boys play on a building site for Corporation housing, a government development which will later bring tensions to Barrytown. The houses are being built on previously open fields that the boys used to explore, hemming them in and robbing them of their unspoilt playground. Moreover, the government housing will later introduce into Paddy's middle-class world families that he finds alien and sometimes threatening. The Corporation housing represents the harsher elements of life that will gradually encroach on his childhood innocence. Note that the narrative of *Paddy Clarke Ha Ha Ha* is multi-layered throughout, so that the reader, complicit with Doyle, can understand elements of Paddy's story more fully than he does. This technique creates an ironic awareness in the reader of the innocence that Paddy will soon lose.

SECTION 3
(pp. 8–9)

Focus on: childish brutality

ANALYSE AND COMPARE . . .

— Doyle has said that one of his intentions in *Paddy Clarke Ha Ha Ha* was to show 'the brutality of childhood'. This episode in which the boys force Sinbad to take lighter fuel in his mouth and then light it is typical of Doyle's treatment of childish brutality, in the way that it manages to make actual cruelty both shocking and humorous. Analyse how Doyle manipulates the tensions in the reader's responses to this episode. Golding's *Lord of the Flies* (1954) was an influence on his treatment of the theme of the brutality of childhood. If it interests you to do a comparison with Golding's novel, refer to the Contexts section (p. 151).

SECTION 4
(pp. 9–10)

Focus on: religion

GAUGE THE TONE . . .

— This section includes the first explicit reference in the novel to religion: 'We'd draw a man on the paper and burn holes in him; in his hands and his feet, like Jesus. We drew long hair on him. We left his mickey [penis] till last' (p. 9). What does the tone of this brief allusion suggest about Paddy's attitude to religion? For a fuller discussion of Doyle's treatment of religion in *Paddy Clarke Ha Ha Ha*, refer to the Contexts section (pp. 154–155).

SECTION 5
(pp. 10–11)

Focus on: father and son

INTERPRET THE DIALOGUE . . .
— Here we see Paddy with his father in an episode that is written almost entirely in dialogue. Doyle shows the relationship between father and son but stops short of explaining it. Typically, he expects the reader to read between the lines. What are the benefits of this technique? Interpret the dialogue: what impression do you form of the relationship between father and son in this section?

SECTIONS 6–7
(pp. 11–15)

Focus on: truth and lies

DETERMINE AND DISCUSS . . .
— A number of lies and half-truths are told and discussed in these sections. What does the narrator regard as lying, and how does he regard the lies that others tell? Pick out the different versions of truth and lying that you are given here. Do children usually have a more flexible view of the truth than adults have, in your opinion?

SECTIONS 8–10
(pp. 15–24)

Focus on: narrative technique

NOTE THE CONNECTIONS . . .

— In these sections Paddy's narrative meanders between various episodes set in different places and at different times. Note how many different topics his ten-year-old mind moves between, then look at how he makes connections between them. What do these connections suggest about how his mind works?

— There are also several instances in this section of allusions, which are another kind of connection (see the Glossary for a fuller definition). Instances of such allusions are to the popular 1960s television series *Voyage to the Bottom of the Sea*; Belvedere, a Roman Catholic school in Dublin which Stephen Dedalus attends in Joyce's *A Portrait of the Artist as a Young Man* (1916); the Corporation, the government body charged with building the new housing in Dublin mentioned earlier; the 1916 Proclamation of Independence; and Norman Mailer's World War II novel *The Naked and the Dead* (1948). The reader's understanding of these allusions is likely to be more mature than Paddy's. That is, the narrative is again working on two levels, one reflecting what goes on inside his head and the other speaking to the reader over his head, emphasising the ironic gap between Paddy's view of the world and an adult's.

— To see how this technique works in more detail, you might do some brief research into the 1916 Easter Rising and the Proclamation of Independence (see the Contexts section on pp. 158–160), then compare your findings with Paddy's reactions to Miss Watkins's lesson two years earlier on pp. 20–3.

Focus on: the Irish language

NOTE AND RESEARCH . . .

— Note the deliberate and rather stilted use of Irish phrases at Paddy's school. For many years after independence, Irish continued to be taught in schools, despite the fact that many of the teachers spoke it no better than their charges. By 1968, the time when *Paddy Clarke Ha Ha Ha* is set, the small area in the west of Ireland where Irish was spoken as a first language (called Gaeltacht) had a population of only some 32,000. To research the decline of Irish further, read J. J. Lee's *Ireland 1912–1985: Politics and Society* (1990). The inclusion of occasional Irish phrases has the ironic effect of presenting it as a dead language. Doyle says something about this in the interview (pp. 16–17)

SECTION 11
(pp. 24–30)

Focus on: father and son

ANALYSE THE DIALOGUE . . .

— Paddy attempts to understand some complex current affairs, and his father tries to explain them in a way that will make sense. What does this dialogue contribute to your understanding of a) Paddy's character, b) Paddy's father's character, c) their relationship, and d) the ironies created by the gap between Paddy's childish view of the world and his father's adult view?

Focus on: religion

COMMENT . . .

— There are numerous references to religion in this episode, all of which somehow connect it with strife. One of the less obvious is the comment, 'I didn't get it, fully, what he'd said,

but it was the kind of thing that Ma didn't like him saying'
(p. 26). This reference is significant, because it foreshadows the
troubles in the parents' marriage that will dominate the last
part of the novel, in which their contrasting religious beliefs
are an additional source of tension. What impression of religion does Doyle create in this section?

SECTIONS 12–13
(pp. 30–3)

Focus on: nostalgia

ANALYSE . . .
— Bearing in mind that the novel will later trace the painful
breakdown of Paddy's family, how does Doyle make use of
nostalgia – the sentimental desire for what is past and irrecoverable – in this section?

Focus on: physical sensation

COMPARE . . .
— Compare Paddy's sensitivity to physical sensation on p. 33
with that of the very young Stephen Dedalus in the opening
passage of Joyce's *A Portrait of the Artist as a Young Man* (1916).
If you read on in Joyce for the next seventeen pages or so (up
to 'and silently past the people who knelt by the water's edge'),
you could broaden your comparison to how the two boys relate
to their peers at school and how they try to make sense of the
adult world, especially of religious and political issues in Ireland,
in the two novels so far. Both novels make use of the colours
red and green. You will see that whereas in *A Portrait of the
Artist as a Young Man* these colours symbolise the two sides in
the Irish struggle for independence (green being associated with

121

Republicanism, red with Ulster), Paddy associates red, not with politics, but with Manchester United. This may be a political point in itself, about the English influence on the culture of contemporary Dublin.

SECTIONS 14–17
(pp. 34–42)

Focus on: tensions

DETERMINE . . .
— Pick out the different kinds of tension that emerge in Sections 14, 16 and 17. How fully does Paddy understand a) the social tensions, and b) the marital tensions that he witnesses?

Focus on: the grotesque

REFLECT . . .
— Section 16 (pp. 38–41) contains several references to physically grotesque images: a spongy nose, varicose veins, farting and snoring; and it finishes with an image of boys swinging like apes from a tree, shouting a rhyme about having a 'hairy gee [genitals, usually used of a woman]'. These references in part reflect a young boy's natural delight in all things physical, but it is also an example of how Doyle regularly uses realism for its humorous potential. Why is the human body and its functions potentially so funny? Might it be that humour is often a defensive reaction to things that we find difficult to accept – our vulnerability to accident, ageing and death – a shared way of diffusing our common fear of the dangers and pains that life holds? To help you to answer these questions,

you might refer to the exercises on 'realism' and on 'the comic perspective' in the Contexts section (p. 150 and p. 154).

SECTIONS 18–22
(pp. 42–59)

Focus on: humour

ANALYSE THE COMPLICITY . . .
— Paddy is an inquisitive child who tries to understand the world by asking questions about it, by remembering stories and indiscriminately collecting any other odd scraps of interesting information that he can find. His observations are often so naive, and his earnest attempts to list his knowledge so artless, that although Paddy's displays of what he knows in these sections are not meant to be humorous, they end up being unwittingly so. Conversely, have there been any details in the novel so far that Paddy has found funny, but you have not? Consider the ways in which Doyle sets up a complicity between himself and the reader, in some or all of these sections, so that we can enjoy the humour at Paddy's expense.

Focus on: storytelling

ASSESS . . .
— Look at Paddy's account of the story of Father Damien in Section 21 on pp. 46–53. We have seen already that he enjoys words; now we see his pleasure in telling a story. Does he tell it well? Assess his storytelling skills.

Focus on: religion

INTERPRET . . .
— Read closely Paddy's parents' responses to his announcement

that he has a vocation (pp. 52–3). Interpret what their responses indicate about their contrasting attitudes to religion.

SECTIONS 23–4
(pp. 59–61)

Focus on: anxiety

CONSIDER AND APPLY . . .

— The novelist and short-story writer Susan Hill has often written about children. She has said that she sees childhood as an anxious time: 'I think fear in children is grossly underestimated. I think children are always anxious.' What sort of things has Paddy been anxious about so far in the novel? Consider the presentation of Paddy's anxieties, both explicit and implied, on pp. 59–61.

SECTIONS 25–6
(pp. 61–6)

Focus on: adults and children

RESPOND . . .

— Although Paddy doesn't like Mr Hennessey, he is used to the teacher's bullying manner and seems to accept it. What does it say about the ethos of the school that a teacher is allowed to abuse his power over the children as 'Henno' does, and what effects are this sort of adult-child relationship likely to have on the children's view of what is normal and acceptable? How do you respond to Mr Hennessey's actions on pp. 61–5? Write him a letter, telling him whether you think he is any good as a teacher, and why.

COMPARE . . .

— Hennessey's treatment of his charges is juxtaposed with the account of Paddy's mother's loving response to Francis's crying. Look at the way she responds to Francis and then analyse the effects that are created by placing these two episodes side by side.

SECTION 27
(pp. 67–72)

Focus on: the untold story

NOTICE . . .

'One of the eyes was blacked, like Missis Byrne's on our road' (p. 67). Paddy is too innocent to guess that Missis Byrne is a victim of domestic violence, but the reader is likely to pick up Doyle's implication. Doyle wrote a television series called *The Family* which was aired on the BBC in 1994, and which caused a furore in Ireland for its bleak representation of family life. One of the characters from this series, Paula Spencer, was a victim of domestic violence. Although not a major character in *The Family*, Paula interested Doyle so much that he gave her a voice in his fifth novel, *The Woman Who Walked Into Doors* (1996). In this novel Paula recounts the story of her marriage to Charlo, and the eighteen years of physical abuse she suffered at his hands until she finally retaliated. Part of the paradox of her awful situation is that she longs for other people to notice the signs of her abuse so that she can tell them everything, but even so, out of shame and fear, she purposely keeps the abuse a secret. If you read *The Woman Who Walked Into Doors*, Missis Byrne's very brief and silent appearance on the fringes of *Paddy Clarke Ha Ha Ha* will leave you with an awareness that she too has a story that has gone untold.

Focus on: control

IDENTIFY AND CONSIDER . . .
— This section draws together a variety of Paddy's memories. Running through them is the idea of control, and behaviours that break out of control. Look through the section and identify each point at which this idea is suggested. Why is the idea of breaking out of control so interesting to children, do you think?

SECTION 28
(pp. 72–5)

Focus on: death and fire

REFLECT AND APPLY . . .
— Doyle has said that adults tend to sentimentalise children. This episode shows the fascination that many children, perhaps especially boys, have with death and with fire. Both ideas have occurred before (see pp. 1 and 9, for instance). Do you agree that children are fascinated by death and fire; and if so, why is this, do you think?

SECTION 29
(pp. 75–6)

Focus on: books and authors

NOTICE . . .
— Paddy's parents both read. On p. 24 his father was reading Norman Mailer's novel *The Naked and the Dead*, and on p. 61 Paddy says that his mother reads regularly. The books that he

uses for his game in this section are *Ivanhoe* (1819), one of the 'Waverley' novels by the Scottish writer Sir Walter Scott, a chivalric romance set in the reign of Richard I; and Graham Greene's novel *Our Man in Havana* (1958). What do these allusions suggest about the level of education of Paddy's family? Paddy himself likes words, is fascinated by stories and has a strong imagination. Although Doyle denies that Paddy Clarke is a self-portrait, there are obvious links – not least that Doyle was also ten in 1968 and grew up in a middle-class family in the Dublin suburbs.

SECTION 30
(pp. 76–83)

Focus on: games

REFLECT . . .

— The children play a game that combines competition with the thrill of danger – the possibility of being caught and punished. It also includes an element of taunting adults that some children relish. Doyle did not play this game as a child (he heard about it from children he later taught), but he has said that he wished he had. Think about children's games generally, and make a list of the aspects that children seem to enjoy most in their games. What do these reveal about children? Has Doyle successfully portrayed these qualities of childhood?

SECTIONS 31–4
(pp. 83–90)

Focus on: inherited stories

RESEARCH AND ASSESS . . .

— These sections juxtapose two kinds of inherited stories: Paddy's father's favourite Irish folk ballads, most of which here are about marital strife; and Roman Catholic doctrine on Heaven, Hell and Purgatory. Although Paddy explains Roman Catholic doctrine in simplistic terms, his summary is essentially accurate. Research these teachings on the afterlife in more detail yourself. How do you react to these doctrinal teachings? Do you find them frightening or reassuring? Helpful, or manipulative? Sympathetic to human experience, or harsh?

— As his family falls apart, Paddy finds no solace from religion ('I didn't pray; there were no prayers for this,' he says of his parents' arguments on p. 154). What point is Doyle implicitly making about Roman Catholic teaching and its capacity to help in ordering experience, by placing it next to the episodes featuring folk ballads about marital breakdown, do you think?

SECTION 35
(pp. 90–6)

Focus on: realism

READ AND IDENTIFY . . .

— This section brilliantly evokes an unsuccessful family outing of a kind that most people will immediately recognise. In its truth to common experience and in its focus on commonplace details, this section is an example of Doyle's 'realism'. Look this term up in the Glossary and refer to the exercise on 'realism' in the Contexts section (p. 150). Then read the section carefully and identify ten details that, for you, make this section 'realistic'.

SECTIONS 36–7
(pp. 96–103)

Focus on: comedy

CREATE . . .

— The episode of the boys getting their BCG jab (a vaccine which protects against meningeal tuberculosis) is carefully structured and contains all the elements of a comic set piece: the build-up of anticipation; the focus on the human body and on the boys' humiliation; the sexual overtones; even the minor detail (a safety pin) which is introduced in advance and forgotten, only to return awkwardly at the moment of greatest embarrassment – all of these contribute. Using Doyle's episode as a model, write a comic scene of your own which uses some or all of the elements mentioned above.

SECTIONS 38–41
(pp. 103–13)

Focus on: images

ANALYSE THE EFFECTS . . .

— One of the ways in which these sections are linked is that they all feature images of enclosed spaces: the safety of a space under a table, or of a room seen through a window at night, or behind a locked door when an angry neighbour comes calling; the hole the boys would like to sink into as a sanctuary from the headmaster's questioning; the pipes and spaces on the old bridge where the boys could hide, safe from their chasers. These spaces offer sanctuary – dark places to hide away in. Not all enclosed spaces are sanctuaries, however, they can be threatening and suffocating: the sewer is smelly and dirty, and we hear of two workmen who supposedly drowned in 'muck'. Analyse the various ways in which Doyle has used these images of enclosed spaces to play on ideas of threat and of sanctuary. Note that these images occur at the point in the novel where Paddy is becoming aware of the insecurity in his parents' marriage.

SECTION 42
(pp. 113–21)

Focus on: territory

ACCOUNT FOR . . .
— The descriptions of the boys playing outside are full of images of freedom, but also of the threat posed to their sense of territory by the encroaching Corporation houses and their inhabitants. What seems to be Paddy's attitude to the presence of the Corporation house children? Look in particular at the way he treats the lone stranger on pp. 120–1. Account for Paddy's actions, bearing in mind his emotional make-up and his experiences of increasing insecurity in the novel so far.

CREATE . . .
— Retell the episode on pp. 120–1 from the point of view of the boy who wants to play football with Paddy's group. Be sure to convey his thoughts and feelings, both before offering to join in and after being excluded by Paddy. What effect is created in the novel by the absence of his point of view?

SECTIONS 43–4
(pp. 121–5)

Focus on: physical sensation

IDENTIFY AND EVALUATE . . .
— Paddy delights in physical sensations. Look closely at these sections and identify the various images of sensation, applying to all of the physical senses. How successfully does Doyle convey sensuous experience, in your opinion?

SECTIONS 45–6
(pp. 125–7)

Focus on: the family

DISCUSS . . .
— 'I'd saved Sinbad' (p. 126). Previously, Paddy has claimed to hate Sinbad, and he has been persistently unkind to him earlier in the novel. Although his parents still treat Paddy very much as a child (for example, on p. 125), in some ways he is growing up and assuming increasing responsibility for the family's happiness. In what ways is 'the family' central to Paddy's sense of security?

SECTIONS 47–8
(pp. 127–33)

Focus on: inclusion and exclusion

WEIGH UP . . .
— The boys tolerate the pain of being hit with a poker by

Kevin during their mock-religious ceremonies because 'It was good being in the circle, better than where Liam was going' (p. 131). The bizarre ceremony is a ritual test of strength and courage, but paradoxically it requires an abject willingness to endure unnecessary pain. Paddy does this; Liam walks away. Do you agree with Paddy's claim that 'I was the real hero, not Liam' (p. 132)?

Focus on: the word 'fuck'

READE CLOSELY . . .

— Read carefully the paragraph on p. 132 that starts 'Fuck was always too loud'. What does the imagery Paddy uses to describe the experience of saying this word reveal about his sensitivity to language and his feel for the power of language? Note that the words 'sensitivity' and 'feel' point to the way Paddy experiences language physically.

SECTIONS 49–50
(pp. 133–7)

Focus on: authorial disinterest

EXAMINE THE TECHNIQUE . . .

— 'It was only printing and my da was a liar' (p. 137). The reader will probably see the father's lie as harmless, even as a kindness; but it seems to be a revelation for Paddy which damages his faith in his father and breaks their previously unperplexed closeness. Doyle represents the gradual breakdown of trust in the family without judging any of the characters, and with striking authorial disinterest (not interchangeable with 'uninterest'). How does he control the reader's response to this lying incident so that we see neither Paddy nor his father as culpable?

SECTIONS 51–2
(pp. 137–40)

Focus on: divisions

SPOT THE PATTERN . . .

— Whenever we have seen Paddy's relationship with his mother in the novel she has come across as a loving, nurturing and sympathetic character. The episode on pp. 137–40 is no exception. However, we see here that she is not without prejudices. She snobbishly insists on calling the front room a 'drawing room' (p. 137); and she betrays some racial and spiritual arrogance when she asks Paddy if he'd like to go to Africa 'To convert the black babies' (p. 139). Notice the emphasis on p. 140 on the increasing difficulty of open communication between the family members. Bearing these ideas in mind, and thinking back over the novel so far, how is Doyle gradually building up a pattern of images of divisions and tensions where before none was evident?

SECTIONS 53–6
(pp. 140–6)

Focus on: cruelty

RELATE . . .

— Considering that Paddy likes dogs and wants one, why does he behave cruelly towards Benson? Relate this incident to the theme of cruelty in the novel as a whole.

Focus on: knowing

NOTICE . . .

— A small child 'knows' the world through touch, and only

133

later begins to understand it through ideas. How is the theme of the different ways of knowing, and of the difficulties of knowing things clearly, developed on pp. 140–6?

SECTIONS 57–9
(pp. 146–53)

Focus on: a child's-eye view

GAUGE THE IRONY . . .
— From p. 1, where Paddy says that 'having a dead ma' would be 'brilliant, wouldn't it?', Doyle creates an ironic gap between a child's view and an adult's view of the world for the reader to enjoy. How does he employ the irony between Paddy's and the reader's views of freedom, glamour and danger on pp. 146–9?

Focus on: territory

ANALYSE THE DICTION . . .
— Analyse the kinds of language that Paddy uses to talk about his gang's 'territory' in this section. What does this diction reveal about how he thinks of the area they play on, and of the new Corporation housing?

SECTION 60
(pp. 153–5)

Focus on: religion

EXAMINE AND INFER . . .
— As his parents' marriage disintegrates, Paddy finds no solace in religion. Examine Paddy's reaction to his father's failure to

observe the rules about the stipulated period of fasting before Mass, and see if you can draw any conclusions about what religion 'means' to Paddy at this stage in the novel.

SECTIONS 61–3
(pp. 155–65)

Focus on: crime and punishment

EVALUATE . . .
— Look for and list all the 'crimes' that the characters are guilty of in Section 62 (pp. 155–63). Consider which is the worst, and why, among these three: a child shoplifts something he doesn't much want for the thrill of it; a group of boys forces another boy to eat washing powder; a father hits his children with a belt as a punishment. Who is guilty and who is innocent? Notice how Paddy's sense of values is getting blurred as he grows out of childhood. In particular, look at his own confusion about who is to blame, especially in his deteriorating relationship with his parents. As this relationship becomes more complex in these sections, what is happening to his relationship with Sinbad?

SECTIONS 64–6
(pp. 165–73)

Focus on: separations and divisions

GENERALISE . . .
— 'I was better than them. Separate, it was different' (p. 167). Look at how many distinctions and evaluations Paddy makes in these sections. Look also at how his language is increasingly

suggestive of conflict. Consider the validity of the claim that in the novel so far growing up is presented as a process of gradual separation from others, of becoming aware of differences and conflicts.

Focus on: soccer and the English

CONSIDER . . .

— Note that the boys follow English teams and idolise English players. Doyle stresses the influence of English culture in Dublin throughout his work. What is it in particular about soccer – both playing it and supporting adult teams – that so appeals to these boys? You might consider the ways in which soccer formalises conflict, deepening a sense of divisions, differences and team loyalties, at the same time as making these divisions socially acceptable, even safe.

SECTION 67
(pp. 173–6)

Focus on: disorientation

ANALYSE THE METAPHOR . . .

— Paddy has spent most of the novel trying to 'orientate' himself: to learn about the world and about who he is in relation to it. This section shows him both trying to orientate himself (by making sense of experience) and disorientating himself by spinning. Does this image lend itself to interpretation as a metaphor for Paddy's relationship to his world at this stage in the novel?

SECTIONS 68–9
(pp. 176–80)

Focus on: order and disorder

INFER . . .

— What is happening to Paddy's world? Consider why it matters so much to Paddy that the family's domestic routines should stay constant and reliable.

Focus on: offstage

IMAGINE AND CREATE . . .

— It's a characteristic of a first-person narrative that their view of events is restricted to what the narrator knows or notices. The reader is aware that much of the action of *Paddy Clarke Ha Ha Ha* is happening 'offstage'. What do you imagine is the source of the tension between Paddy's parents? What do they argue about? And how do they each feel about the steady disintegration of their marriage? Create either a narrative or a script which shows an argument that they have 'offstage'. Then consider what effects Doyle achieves by keeping such arguments out of the narrative.

SECTION 70
(pp. 180–7)

Focus on: fighting

DISCUSS . . .

— '—No kicking, said the workman. —That's not the way to fight' (p. 186). Discuss the idea that the boys' friendships and antagonisms are governed by a set of unspoken but under-stood rules. What does it show about Charles Leavy that he does not obey these rules?

SECTIONS 71–2
(pp. 187–90)

Focus on: anger

INFER . . .

— When his father asks Sinbad, '—Why do you do these things? Why are you doing them?', Sinbad answers, '—The devil tempts me' (p. 189). What hints are there that their father is aware that the boys' increasingly delinquent behaviour, far from being wicked, is a normal response to a distressing situation?

SECTION 73
(p. 190)

Focus on: domestic violence

RESEARCH AND DISCUSS . . .

— Most married couples have disagreements; luckily, only a very small minority resort to physical violence. How widespread is the problem of domestic violence? Research it on the Internet using a search engine. Doyle drew attention to the issue of domestic violence in his 1994 BBC series *The Family*, to the anger of many viewers who said he was misrepresenting family life, and again in *The Woman Who Walked Into Doors* (1996) – see the exercise for Section 27 above. Consider and discuss the following statistics from the United States during the period in which Doyle wrote these fictions:

● 'Over two-thirds of violent victimizations against women were committed by someone known to them: Approximately 28% were intimates such as husbands or boyfriends. Almost 6 times as many women victimized by intimates (18%) as those victimized by strangers (3%) did not report their violent victimization to police because they feared reprisal from the offender.' (Ronet Bachman, PhD, US Department of Justice Bureau of Statistics, 'Violence Against Women: A National Crime Victimization Survey Report', January 1994, p. 1)

- 'Battered women seek medical attention for injuries sustained as a consequence of domestic violence significantly more often after separation than during cohabitation; about 75% of the visits to emergency rooms by battered women occur after separation.' (Stark and Flitcraft, 1988)

- 'There are 1,500 shelters for battered women in the United States. There are 3,800 animal shelters' (Schneider, 1990)

- 'Violence is the reason stated for divorce in 22% of middle-class marriages.' (EAP Digest, November/December 1991)

— See also the exercise on 'Domestic Violence' in the Contexts section (pp. 156–7). Consider why the moment when Paddy's father hits his mother is so much more significant than any of their previous arguments.

SECTION 74
(pp. 191–6)

Focus on: Keith Simpson

ASSESS THE EFFECTS . . .

— The story of Keith Simpson's death is a mini-narrative that takes place on the sidelines of Paddy's life. He is aware of it, but Keith was not a friend ('He was from the Corporation houses'), and Keith's tragedy does not impact much on Paddy, who is caught up with his own family's problems. The reader might react differently to this side story, however, and feel great sympathy for the family whose tragedy – made worse, perhaps, by the fact it was an accident – is going on close by. Note that many of the peripheral details that Doyle uses to give Paddy's story a context focus on the ways in which people confront life's difficulties in family situations (there are more instances in the next section). We are reminded that a circumstance like Paddy's is just one of many that people face, and by no means the most painful. Assess the effects created by the tangential inclusion of Keith's story at this point in the novel.

SECTION 75
(pp. 196–202)

Focus on: casual violence

LIST, ASSESS AND RELATE . . .
— List the incidents of casual violence in this section, and assess what it reveals about the boys who inflict it. Relate it to the portrayal of violence in the novel so far.

SECTIONS 76–7
(pp. 202–11)

Focus on: parents and children

TRANSFORM . . .
— We have never got close to Paddy's father – we are not even told his name – and our view of him is partly coloured by Paddy's perceptions. Give the father a 'voice'. Transform Section 76 (pp. 202–8) into an interior monologue by Paddy's father, in which you tell the events recorded here from his point of view.

140

READ BETWEEN THE LINES AND COMMENT . . .

— What is going on under the surface of the episode on pp. 208–11? Read it carefully, analyse what is going on between the lines (what are his parents really thinking?) and then write a commentary which explains your conclusions.

SECTIONS 78–9
(pp. 211–16)

Focus on: brothers

EXPLAIN . . .

— Explain Paddy's attitude towards Sinbad in the two episodes on pp. 211–16. Has his attitude developed during the novel?

SECTIONS 80–7
(pp. 216–25)

Focus on: keeping watch

DISCUSS . . .

— Most of these sections trace the final disintegration of Paddy's parents' marriage. Paddy has tried in the past to intervene, to make things 'nice' (p. 211), but increasingly he feels impotent, and he becomes just a spectator to his parents' conflict. The novel is partly about the pain that parents at war inflict on their children. Discuss what pp. 216–25 contribute towards this theme.

SECTIONS 88–91
(pp. 225–39)

Focus on: getting caught

APPLY . . .

— 'That was what school was all about, not being caught and watching others get caught instead' (pp. 227–8). How does this idea inform Paddy's actions during these sections (both in and out of school)?

SECTIONS 92–4
(pp. 239–43)

Focus on: Paddy and Francis

UNPICK THE COMPLEXITIES . . .

Look at these quotations from p. 240:

- He frightened me.
- He could stop everything happening, and I couldn't.
- I wanted to kill him.
- All I wanted to do was help him and he wouldn't let me.

— Try to unpick the contradictions and complexities in Paddy's feelings towards his brother. Write three hundred words to explain them.

SECTION 95
(pp. 243–5)

Focus on: divorce

PLACE IN A POLITICAL CONTEXT . . .

— Paddy's parents do not hate each other: they simply cannot live together happily. However, the alternatives facing them in Ireland in 1968 were bleak. Divorce was illegal, so they either had to struggle on unhappily, with the threat of physical abuse (like Mrs Shiels on p. 245), or to have an illicit relationship with someone they could never marry (like Mrs Swanwick on p. 245), or to separate and live without a partner. In what ways might Doyle's portrayal of this unhappy marriage be said to be political? You should refer to the exercises on 'divorce' and 'politics' in the Contexts section (pp. 155–156) for some further ideas on this topic.

SECTIONS 96–9
(pp. 245–53)

Focus on: Charles Leavy

EXAMINE . . .

— Read these sections carefully and consider why Paddy admires Charles Leavy so much. How do you react to Leavy's character? Compare the way Paddy regards Leavy with his reaction to the Corporation house boy on pp. 120–1. What has brought about the change in his attitudes?

SECTIONS 100–4
(pp. 253–67)

Focus on: confusion

ANALYSE AND RESPOND . . .
— Examine the ways in which Paddy expresses his confusion during these sections. In particular, how does Doyle convey Paddy's loneliness?
— How do you react to Paddy at this stage in the novel? Consider how successfully Doyle manipulates your reactions, and with what technical literary means.

Focus on: the child's perspective

CONSIDER . . .
— Consider the claim that by presenting an adult problem – marital discord – through a child's eyes, Doyle succeeds in depicting the ordinary pains of loss and grief in fresh ways that reflect their true nature.

SECTIONS 105–6
(pp. 267–74)

Focus on: Kevin

MAKE A JUDGMENT . . .
— Kevin has been Paddy's friend for most of the novel. Here they fight angrily. To what extent is Paddy guilty of betraying their friendship?

SECTIONS 107–8
(pp. 274–7)

Focus on: isolation

ASSESS THE EFFECTS . . .
— What effects are created by the juxtaposition of Paddy's isolation at school with his mother's solicitations. Is he still a child, or not? With whom can he communicate now?

SECTIONS 109–14
(pp. 277–82)

Focus on: the end

GAUGE THE MOOD . . .
— What is the mood of the ending? The final section shows Paddy and his father continuing to meet, but the mood of the meeting is distant, formal and stilted. The taunting chant that precedes it is a reminder of the cruelty that has echoed throughout the novel. Paddy's dreams of the glamour of escape were only dreams – the final scenes are the grim reality. How hopeful is the novel, in the end?

Looking over the whole novel

QUESTIONS FOR DISCUSSION OR ESSAYS
1. 'Doyle never judges his characters, but forgives them everything.' Discuss.

2. 'Doyle manages to create humour without ever undermining the seriousness of the issues his characters face.' Have

you found this to be true of *Paddy Clarke Ha Ha Ha*?

3. '*Paddy Clarke Ha Ha Ha* is multi-layered. Behind Paddy Clarke's childish view of the world, Doyle speaks to the reader about adult themes.' Discuss.

4. Examine the importance of 'family' in *Paddy Clarke Ha Ha Ha*.

5. Consider the presentation of the gang mentality in *Paddy Clarke Ha Ha Ha*.

6. How important are 'inclusion' and 'exclusion' in Paddy's world?

7. Discuss the presentation of the theme of friendship in *Paddy Clarke Ha Ha Ha*.

8. What does the novel have to say about innocence, and about its two opposites, guilt and knowledge?

9. Discuss the ways that the novel presents physical violence.

10. How convincingly does Doyle create the consciousness of a ten-year-old boy in *Paddy Clarke Ha Ha Ha*?

11. Consider the ways in which Doyle uses dialogue to create character.

12. Discuss Doyle's use of narrative voice in the creation of Paddy Clarke's character.

13. In what ways might *Paddy Clarke Ha Ha Ha* be described as an 'artful' novel?

14. What does a reading of *Paddy Clarke Ha Ha Ha* suggest about the waning influence of the Roman Catholic Church in Ireland?

15. '*Paddy Clarke Ha Ha Ha* is about a child leaving behind the luxury of irresponsibility.' Discuss.

16. Consider the claim that despite his attempts at being hard, Paddy Clarke is an emotionally sensitive child.

17. How hopeful do you find the ending of *Paddy Clarke Ha Ha Ha*?

Contexts, comparisons and complementary readings

PADDY CLARKE HA HA HA

These sections suggest contextual and comparative ways of reading these works by Doyle. You can put your reading in a social, historical or literary context. You can make comparisons – again, social, literary or historical – with other texts or art works. Or you can choose complementary works (of whatever kind) – that is, art works, literary works, social reportage or facts which in some way illuminate the text by sidelights or interventions which you can make into a telling framework. Some of the suggested contexts are directly connected to the book, in that they will give you precise literary or social frames in which to situate the novel. In turn, these are either related to the period within which the novel is set, or to the time – now – when you are reading it. Some of these examples are designed to suggest books or other texts that may make useful sources for comparison (or for complementary purposes) when you are reading *Paddy Clarke Ha Ha Ha*. Again, they may be related to literary or critical themes, or they may be relevant to social and cultural themes current 'then' or 'now'.

Focus on: 'realism'

READ AND APPLY . . .

— Doyle has said that his job as a novelist is 'to describe things and people as they really are', and that his intention when writing *Paddy Clarke Ha Ha Ha* was to present childhood and family dysfunction in realistic terms. Look up 'realism' in the Glossary. 'The realist is deliberately selective in material and prefers the average, the commonplace and the everyday over the rarer aspects of the social scene. The characters, therefore, are usually of the middle class or (less frequently) the working class – people without exceptional endowments, who live through ordinary experiences of childhood, adolescence, love, marriage, parenthood, infidelity, and death; who find life rather dull and often unhappy, though it may be brightened by touches of beauty and joy' (M. H. Abrams, *A Glossary of Literary Terms*, 1985). According to which of these criteria can *Paddy Clarke Ha Ha Ha* be called a realist novel?

Focus on: literary precursors

COMPARE . . .

— *Paddy Clarke Ha Ha Ha* is a 'coming-of-age' novel, and as such has many precursors. The opening sentence of *Paddy Clarke* echoes the first line of James Joyce's *A Portrait of the Artist as a Young Man* (1916), 'Once upon a time and a very good time it was there was a moocow coming down along the road.' Although Doyle denies any consciously deliberate use of Joyce's influence in this novel (though not on others: he deliberately used Joyce's *Dubliners* and *Ulysses* to help him recreate authentic early twentieth-century Dublin patterns of speech for *A Star Called Henry*), it is questionable whether any contemporary novelist writing about Ireland, and in particular about Dublin, can really escape Joyce's influence. There are obvious points of comparison: both novels portray the childhoods of Irish Catholic Dubliners who live with dysfunctional families; both present protagonists with acute sensibilities, especially to physical sensation, and whose views of the world are conveyed through the styles in which the narratives are written and through the detailing of sense impressions; both characters are fascinated by words; in both novels, the importance of each event and of each character is determined by how important they are to the protagonist; both are mimetic of Dublin speech patterns. However, Joyce's semi-autobiographical novel is more concerned with the influence of the Roman Catholic Church, which barely figures in Paddy's life except as a source of amusement. To make a detailed comparison, read the first two chapters of *A Portrait of the Artist*, which depict Stephen Dedalus's childhood, and compare the ways in which the two novelists evoke a sense of a child's view of the world.

— Doyle has said that William Golding's *Lord of the Flies* (1954), the story of schoolboys who are marooned on a desert island and revert to savagery, was an important influence on *Paddy Clarke Ha Ha Ha*. 'I saw variations on Piggy and all the other characters in my classroom and on my street, and I thought that it was a very true and an honest book, and its real power was that it showed the brutality of childhood. I suppose I was trying to do that as well.' However, Golding's vision is darker than Doyle's; it is informed by a philosophical view of human nature as essentially corrupt and beyond redemption, whereas in Doyle's novels the darker aspects of life are presented with a mixture of realism and humour. Read at least a part of *Lord of the Flies* and compare Golding's portrayal of 'the brutality of childhood' with Doyle's.

— Paddy has been compared to Huck Finn, the eponymous protagonist of Mark Twain's novel *The Adventures of Huckleberry*

Finn (1884): for their inquisitive natures; their perceptiveness; their superstitious rituals; and their premature propulsion into adult life. Moreover, the novels present their narratives through the points of view of children, and both carry this trick off convincingly, while simultaneously offering underlying critiques of adult issues. For a fuller comparison of the two texts, refer to *Reading Roddy Doyle* by Caramine White.

— For another child's-eye view of an unhappy marriage, you might read Part One of D. H. Lawrence's semi-autobiographical coming-of-age novel *Sons and Lovers* (1913). This novel is a fictionalised portrait of the miserable marriage between Lawrence's middle-class, educated mother and his coal miner father. It gives a vivid portrait of the desperation of two people who are locked into an ill-matched marriage that they cannot escape, told from the point of view of one of the children. Compare the way the two novelists present the idea of 'child as observer' of these two marriages.

— Doyle has cited the Dublin writer Flann O'Brien (1911–66) as the greatest influence on his comic vision and style. O'Brien was a master stylist of comic prose, with a cruel vision of the human race as ridiculously petty and pretentious. His two best-known works are *At Swim-Two-Birds* (1939) and *The Third Policeman* (written 1940, published 1967), both macabre works in which many of the funniest scenes and conversations are rooted in human pain, ignominy, humiliation and death. Compare O'Brien's comic vision with Doyle's.

— Richard Ford's novel *Wildlife* (1990) inspired aspects of *Paddy Clarke Ha Ha Ha*. It concerns Joe, who is now an adult, recalling confronting his parents' shortcomings at the age of sixteen. Like Doyle, Ford has an ability to capture distinctive voices. You might like to read *Wildlife* to make a comparison and to think about how Ford influenced Doyle.

Focus on: literary successors

RESEARCH AND COMPARE . . .
— Frank McCourt's *Angela's Ashes* (1996) is an autobiographical story of the novelist's impoverished childhood in Limerick in the 1930s and 1940s. You might compare the way McCourt mixes humour and grim realism with Doyle's similar balancing act.

Focus on: friendship

COMPARE . . .
— Compare the portrayal of friendship among pre-pubescent boys in *Paddy Clarke Ha Ha Ha* with Rob Reiner's 1986 film *Stand by Me*, based on Stephen King's novel *The Body* (1974). The film is a nostalgic coming-of-age drama about four twelve-year-old boys' friendships and misadventures over a summer holiday. How sensitively do the two works depict the friendships between boys of this age?

Focus on: 'Irishness' in novels

EXTEND YOUR READING . . .
— Explore literary representations of 'Irishness' by reading any of the following:
- James Joyce's *Dubliners* (1914), a collection of short stories which evokes Irish social habits, religion and the patterns of ordinary lives.
- Flann O'Brien's *At Swim-Two-Birds* (1939), a wildly comic send-up of Irish literature, culture and the concept of Irishness (see 'the comic perspective' below).

- The novels of William Trevor, such as *Mrs Eckdorf in O'Neill's Hotel* (1969). Trevor is known for depicting the everyday, fragmented lives of the inarticulate. He shares with Doyle an interest in the isolation of marginalised characters and the theme of disintegrating community.

Focus on: the comic perspective

DISCRIMINATE . . .

— Comedy and humour do not mean quite the same thing when applied to literature. Look them up in the Glossary. Doyle's novels present some of the bleaker aspects of life, and his plots show characters meeting the challenges of their lives in a way that is typical of comedy. They are also able to find humour in even the grimmest and most unjust circumstances. His novels are therefore both comic and humorous. However, Doyle's social vision has become steadily darker over the years, so that the humour and optimism of his first two works has gradually become eclipsed by a sense of the overwhelming difficulties in the lives of his characters. Although there is some hope at the end of each novel, the comic aspects of Doyle's work have become less pronounced, and his humour has become grimmer. Look at Caramine White's comments on this topic in the Selected Extracts section (pp. 212–3).

Focus on: religion

EXAMINE . . .

— Like most of Doyle's characters, Paddy Clarke is nominally Roman Catholic, but the Church and its sacraments do not figure importantly in his life. Although there are numerous religious references, Paddy's childish understanding of them suggests that, for him, religion represents a set of arbitrary rules, the breaking of which will be punished severely, but which have little bearing in his mind on questions of right and wrong. Examine the references to prayer, to Mass, to the saints and to the idea of a vocation. An atheist himself, Doyle is critical of the influence of Catholicism in Ireland, which he describes as 'Catholicism without the colour', and does not regret the fact that the influence of the Church on the State has waned in recent years. At no point in the novel does the Church act as a source of reassurance or guidance for Paddy. His parents differ in their views on religion: whereas his mother encourages Paddy in his thoughts about vocation, his father reacts angrily; and perhaps the main way in which religion impacts on Paddy's life is that it is a source of conflict in his family. Examine what Doyle has said about religion in interviews (see pages 221–2 for examples).

Focus on: politics

FIND OUT AND CONSIDER . . .
— Doyle describes himself as socially committed and politically engaged. The television series *Family* was his most political work, which caused widespread discussion about its bleak presentation of family life (see the exercises for Sections 27 and 73). Doyle's work is rarely overtly political, however. Although most of his writing touches on issues of social politics (class struggles, divorce, domestic violence), he sees political correctness as anathema to good writing, especially to satire. His political instincts are socialist, but he does not belong to a political party and he has repeatedly said that fiction should not be a vehicle for the novelist to preach politics. His novels are notably free

from references to the history of the struggle for Irish independence. His family background is largely Republican,
although his grandfather's brothers fought on both sides in the
civil war and Doyle has spoken about his divided inheritance.
Perhaps the most political aspect of Doyle's novels is precisely
his refusal to deal reverently with the political issues that have
traditionally dominated Irish debate. In a sense he has sought
to reinvent Ireland's image, not as a nationalist, rural, conser-
vative, Roman Catholic nation, but as a place reminiscent of
any number of European states. Find out about Doyle's political engagement, using the interview and the Selected extracts
from critical writings in this guide as a starting point.

Focus on: divorce

CONSIDER . . .
— Doyle's treatment of the theme of divorce in *Paddy Clarke
Ha Ha Ha* points to the underlying political vein in his writing.
In 1968, divorce was illegal in Ireland, so Paddy's parents would
not have been able to obtain one. Unless they are reconciled,
which seems unlikely, they face a stark choice between living
alone, or living outside a legal relationship. Paddy as a child
cannot comment on his experience of his parents' separation
in political terms, but the narrative implies Doyle's passionate
interest in the subject: he was a supporter of the divorce referendum in Ireland in the late 1980s, and continued to voice his
support for the 1996 referendum, which passed by a narrow
margin. Consider what *Paddy Clarke Ha Ha Ha* has to say –
beyond what Paddy Clarke himself has to say – about the
subject of divorce.

Focus on: domestic violence

READ AND CREATE . . .

— See the exercise for Section 73 which gives some data on domestic violence. For a fuller treatment of this issue by Doyle, read his novel *The Woman Who Walked Into Doors* (1996).

— Read the following brief poem called 'Discord in Childhood'. It is by D. H. Lawrence (1885–1930), whose own childhood was blighted by the fights between his ill-matched parents.

> Outside the house an ash-tree hung its terrible whips,
> And at night when the wind rose, the lash of the
>   tree
> Shrieked and slashed the wind, as a ship's
> Weird rigging in a storm shrieks hideously.
>
> Within the house two voices arose, a slender lash
> Whistling she-delirious rage, and the dreadful sound
> Of a male thong booming and bruising, until it had
>   drowned
> The other voice in a silence of blood, 'neath the
>   noise of the ash.

— How does Lawrence employ images of sound and of pain in the poem? Note how, although Lawrence is known to have hated his father and to have sided with his mother in their marital strife (see the notes on his novel *Sons and Lovers* in the Contexts section, p. 152), in this poem he presents the discord impartially. Is the same true of Doyle's presentation of Paddy's parents' arguments?

— Create a poem that Paddy might write about his parents' arguments. You might use some of the words and images from the novel, or you might invent your own. You will need to decide whether Paddy would take sides or remain impartial.

Focus on: the Easter Rising

RESEARCH AND COMPARE . . .
— On Easter Monday of 1916, Patrick Pearse, leading a volunteer army, stormed and occupied the General Post Office in Dublin and several other strategic buildings, and declared Ireland a free republic. However, the rising met with poor support from the Irish people, and by Saturday Pearse and his army had surrendered to troops sent in by the British government. The leaders were executed, and inadvertently transformed into martyrs for the Irish Nationalist cause. Research the events of the uprising. You might include in your research both historical and fictional accounts. If you are interested in reading a fictional account by Doyle of the Easter Rising, read pp. 87–148 of *A Star Called Henry*. W. B. Yeats's poem 'Easter 1916' offers a deeply ambivalent response to the events, recognising the new status of Ireland in events that have given birth to 'a terrible beauty'.

Focus on: the 1916 Proclamation of Independence

ANALYSE THE LANGUAGE . . .
— Below is reproduced the full text of the 'Proclamation of the Republic' made by the self-styled Provisional Government on Easter Monday, 24 April 1916, and read from the steps of the General Post Office by Patrick Pearse. Read closely the language used in the proclamation and comment on what it indicates about the way the Provisional Government viewed their cause.

POBLACHT NA h-EIREANN
THE PROVISIONAL GOVERNMENT OF
THE IRISH REPUBLIC TO THE
PEOPLE OF IRELAND

Irishmen and Irishwomen: In the name of God and of the dead generations from which she receives her old tradition of nationhood, Ireland, through us, summons her children to her flag and strikes for her freedom.

Having organized and trained her manhood through her secret revolutionary organization, the Irish Republican Brotherhood, and through her open military organizations, the Irish Volunteers and the Irish Citizen Army, having patiently perfected her discipline, having resolutely waited for the right moment to reveal itself, she now seizes that moment, and, supported by her exiled children in America and by gallant allies in Europe, but relying in the first on her own strength, she strikes in full confidence of victory.

We declare the right of the people of Ireland to the ownership of Ireland, and to the unfettered control of Irish destinies, to be sovereign and indefeasible. The long usurpation of that right by a foreign people and government has not extinguished the right, nor can it ever be extinguished except by the destruction of the Irish people. In every generation the Irish people have asserted their right to national freedom and sovereignty; six times during the past three hundred years they have asserted it in arms. Standing on that fundamental right and again asserting it in arms in the face of the world, we hereby proclaim the Irish Republic as a Sovereign

Independent State. And we pledge our lives and the lives of our comrades-in-arms to the cause of its freedom, of its welfare, and of its exaltation among the nations.

The Irish Republic is entitled to, and hereby claims, the allegiance of every Irishman and Irishwoman. The Republic guarantees religious and civil liberty, equal rights and equal opportunities of all its citizens, and declares its resolve to pursue the happiness and prosperity of the whole nation and of all its parts, cherishing all the children of the nation equally, and oblivious of the differences carefully fostered by an alien government, which have divided a minority in the past.

Until our arms have brought the opportune moment for the establishment of a permanent National Government, representative of the whole people of Ireland and elected by the suffrages of all her men and women, the Provisional Government, hereby constituted, will administer the civil and military affairs of the Republic in trust for the people.

We place the cause of the Irish Republic under the protection of the Most High God, Whose blessing we invoke upon our arms, and we pray that no one who serves that cause will dishonour it by cowardice, inhumanity, or rapine. In this supreme hour the Irish nation must, by its valour and discipline, and by the readiness of its children to sacrifice themselves for the common good, prove itself worthy of the august destiny to which it is called.

Signed on behalf of the Provisional Government, Thomas J. Clarke, Seán MacDiarmada, Thomas MacDonagh, P. H. Pearse, Eamonn Ceannt, James Connolly, Joseph Plunkett.

VINTAGE
LIVING
TEXTS

The Woman Who Walked Into Doors

IN CLOSE-UP

Reading guides for

THE WOMAN WHO WALKED INTO DOORS

BEFORE YOU BEGIN TO READ . . .
— Read the interview with Doyle. You will see there that he identifies a number of themes as techniques in this novel:

- Domestic violence
- Women and men
- Non-linear narrative structure
- Psychological realism

Other themes that may be useful to consider while reading the novel include:

- Children
- Dependence and power
- Identity and self-realisation
- Speaking out

Reading activities: detailed analysis

Focus on: Paula's provenance

REFLECT . . .

— In 1994 the BBC invited Doyle to write a screenplay on a subject of his choice. He chose to write a four-part series about a family in crisis, each part focusing on a specific member of the family over several months. The series started with Charlo Spencer, a violently abusive husband, and ended by focusing on his wife, Paula. *The Family* drew large audiences in Ireland and stirred widespread controversy there. In particular, viewers wanted to know more about Paula, and why she had married Charlo in the first place. Doyle wrote *The Woman Who Walked Into Doors*, his fifth novel, because he felt that Paula had much more to say. 'I had grown very fond of her and very protective of her because she'd been through so much.' He imagined her sitting down and writing about her past. The novel 'lets her explain, to an extent, why she fell in love with this man and why he fell in love with her and it made him something less of a monster as well'. What does this suggest about the way that characters from fiction (and perhaps especially from a television series) can take on a life of their own, so that people begin to think about them as if they were real? In what senses *is* Paula Spencer made real by the fact that people think of her that way?

Focus on: the novel's structure

ASSESS THE EFFECTS . . .

— Paula's account of her life is not structured in a linear or chronological shape but as a series of spirals. Most of the main events of the story are already in the past. Present situations spark off memories, which give rise to recurring images that spark off more memories. Paula confronts her past, and the events that brought her to where and what she is today – a battered wife and a lonely alcoholic – so that she can live with herself in the present. She remembers her happy and secure childhood, family day trips and holidays, her rebellious adolescence, her unhappy teenage schooldays, and her early relationship with Charlo, which was once joyful and passionate. In what ways is a spiral narrative more suited to presenting lived experience than a linear one, do you think?

Focus on: the confessional narrative

COMPARE . . .

— The narrative reads like a kind of confession, written or spoken after the events it records have finished. It raises the question of how reliable the narrator is: can we trust what we are told? In John Fowles's *The Collector* (1963), for instance, where we are given two accounts of the same events, the first is told by an inarticulate young man who suffers from delusions, and is often later contradicted by the second account we read of the same events from a different narrator. Compare the two novels, which share the idea of a narrative that reads partly as a confession, partly as a self-justification. In what ways does this narrative form confer a sense of intimacy with the narrator, or of being given privileged access to private thoughts? *The*

Woman Who Walked Into Doors is told by a woman who herself questions her ability to unpick truth from illusion, but here the emphasis is on the way she creates her own truth – an emotional truth rather than a factual one. Ask yourself, as you read, to whom the narrative is addressed. Is the narrator talking to herself, like a personal diary? Is it addressed to you, the reader? Or could it be a literal confession to someone else? In other words, what difference does it make to your attitudes to the events and characters of a novel if they are written in the form of a confession?

BE AWARE . . .
— Doyle has often said that his decision to tell Paula's story in her own voice posed a huge artistic challenge. Imagining Paula's experiences as an alcoholic and abused woman, one who is unsure of herself, unsure of her status as a woman, and who is recreating herself by reviewing her past, is a daunting challenge, and the novel has been praised for the success with which it creates Paula's complex world view. As you read, be aware of the subtlety with which Doyle creates Paula's world view.

Focus on: the setting

CONTEXTUALISE . . .
— *The Woman Who Walked Into Doors* is set over a period of some thirty years (1960s–90s) in an unidentified, fictional suburb of Dublin, Ireland, which closely resembles the Barrytown suburb in which Doyle set his earlier novels, *The Barrytown Trilogy* and *Paddy Clarke Ha Ha Ha*. Like *The Woman Who Walked Into Doors*, the trilogy also portrays working-class life. The residents of Barrytown are portrayed as an insular bunch, concerned entirely with their own immediate environment and indifferent to the wider issues of Irish history, politics or religion. Doyle records in *Rory and Ita* (2002), his memoir

about his parents, that when his father came to Dublin he found it was 'like being in a different country. The philosophy was anti-Republican, anti-Gaelic, almost anti-Irish.' There is almost no mention in Doyle's early novels of the conflict in Northern Ireland, of the IRA, or of the Ulster Volunteer Force; and other issues of importance to the rest of Ireland, such as the European Union and financial scandals, hardly figure in the lives of his characters.

— Typically, Doyle's working-class characters are enabled to survive lives that are grim and offer little hope for change by the network provided by community, friends and, especially, family. This reliance on family support is an additional reason why violence within the family is so devastating to Paula, and also helps to explain why she is so determined to protect her children from the abuse that she has endured for eighteen years. If you want to gain a fuller picture of working-class life in Barrytown, read any one of *The Barrytown Trilogy*. The characters from these earlier works are sometimes stereotyped, and a comparison between one of these (Sharon Rabbitte in *The Snapper*, for instance, the only other female character whose consciousness Doyle had previously portrayed) and Paula in *The Woman Who Walked into Doors* highlights the increasing complexity with which Doyle has realised his characters.

CHAPTER I
(pp. 1–2)

Focus on: Paula's voice

LISTEN CAREFULLY . . .
— Paula is representative of many of the problems facing Ireland's poor, but she is also a unique and fully realised character. The chief method Doyle uses to create her complex

character is her voice: she tells her own story in her own idiom, without authorial judgement. This allows the reader to get to know Paula gradually, to accept and understand her. She is not an 'artful' narrator, but gives away details about herself unknowingly. Much is left unexplained, and the reader must continually try to make sense of fragments and clues. As you read the first chapter, pay attention to her 'voice': to the rhythms, to the language she uses, and to the attitudes she reveals towards herself and towards others. What are your first impressions of Paula's character from this opening?

CHAPTER 2
(pp. 3–4)

Focus on: seeds

SPOT THE IRONIES AND THEIR EFFECTS . . .

— Paula's first memories of Charlo convey her sexual attraction towards him. What exactly about him appeals to her so much? The sexual attraction between them is based on a model of his power and her passivity. What hints are there at their first meeting that the aspects of Charlo that make her so attracted to him, and the aspects of Paula that make her want to give herself over to him, are the very things that will enable his later violence towards her? Readers will only become aware of these hints when they have read on and seen how their relationship develops, and the effect is of an irony that is proleptic – which means 'anticipating'. Note how many images and words in this chapter ironically suggest Charlo's later physical abuse of Paula. What is the effect of these proleptic ironies: do they show how good the relationship between Paula and Charlo was at the beginning, and give a measure of how far it later breaks down? Or are they suggesting that in a patriarchal culture even normal and acceptable social conventions contain the seeds which can lead to men abusing women.

CHAPTER 3
(p. 5)

Focus on: perspectives

ANALYSE THE EFFECTS . . .

— Note how this brief chapter, coming immediately after Paula's account of her first meeting with Charlo, alters our perspective of it. However, the crucial action – Charlo hitting Paula – is not shown, but remains only implied, unspoken, hidden from our perspective. What is the effect of this? Analyse how this scene plays on the notion of altered perspectives in other ways. For instance, what effects are created by her perspective of him standing over her? And what is his implied perspective on what he has just done? Note that the whole narrative technique – Paula gives her own account of her past – is the result of her trying to get a clear perspective on the events of her life. The idea of subjective perspectives runs throughout the novel.

CHAPTER 4
(pp. 5–19)

Focus on: the past and the present

LIST AND INTERPRET . . .

— Memories are notoriously unreliable, and even some of Paula's most vivid memories are called into question by Carmel's contradictory accounts of their childhood home. Their contrasting memories will become pronounced later, when we see the importance to Paula of making sense of the present through her past. Although these uncertainties call into question the reliability of Paula's account, the main effect is to emphasise not her unreliability but her honest struggle to find her own truth. What we see in this chapter is Paula using her imagination to give shape and order to her memories; to tell a story about her past that satisfies her need to make sense of her present life as an adult. What impression do the stories she tells in this chapter give you of her childhood home? Read the chapter through carefully and select ten separate words, phrases or images that sum up the mood of her memories of her home. Then find five adjectives of your own to describe this mood. What do Paula's memories indicate about what her childhood means to her now, as a thirty-nine-year-old?

REMEMBER AND COMPARE . . .
— How reliable is your own memory? Write down five mini stories (of a few lines each) from your childhood that sum up for you the mood of various experiences up to the age of about twelve. How clearly do you remember them? Try testing your account by showing these stories to someone else (perhaps a member of your family) who shared the experiences, and ask them whether their memories accord with yours. Does this comparison reveal anything surprising about the reliability of memory?

CHAPTER 5
(pp. 19–20)

Focus on: Paula's kindness

FIND AND RELATE . . .
— Gerard has come to tell Paula some bad news, and she has

already guessed what the news is – 'It clicked inside me when I opened the door' (p. 1). Who is comforting whom in the conversation on pp. 19–20? There are early indications here that Paula is a sympathetic, kind and emotionally giving person. Relate these qualities to what she has told us about her relationships with her parents and with her children in the previous chapter.

CHAPTER 6
(pp. 20–3)

Focus on: reality and imagination

IDENTIFY AND REFLECT . . .

— This chapter sets up a contrast between Paula's memory of the hard reality of her experiences when she first met Charlo and a world in her imagination which is warmer and richer, both physically and emotionally, into which she escapes. Wearing warm and expensive coats; making love with gorgeous movie stars on picnic rugs; warm houses, warm showers and being rich, all figure in this imaginary world. What were the truths about her experiences? Find five images in this chapter that convey these. We see that right from the start of her relationship with Charlo, Paula was always trying to transform the harshness of the truth into something better in her imagination. Do you see this habit of trying to transform reality – 'making it nice' (p. 22) – as a sign of emotional strength or weakness in Paula?

CHAPTER 7
(p. 23)

Focus on: men and women

FIND A PATTERN AND INTERPRET . . .

— The italicised typography of this brief chapter links it in a mini narrative with Chapter 3, where Paula recalls coming round after Charlo had hit her, and his pretence that she had just fallen over. Here, Paula remembers a typical scene later, at the hospital, in which a doctor, inspecting her injuries, notices that she is drunk. The implication is that he puts her injuries down to a drunken accident, and thus makes Paula to blame for them. Why might the doctor make a deliberate decision to ignore his suspicion that she is a victim of domestic violence? Is it significant that the doctor is a man? Why does Paula not say to the doctor that she is being abused and ask him for help, do you think? In both chapters, Paula's suffering is invalidated, even suppressed, by men. This chapter broadens the theme of the abuse of women by men beyond a single violent marriage: the implication is that the abuse of women by men is ignored, and therefore condoned, by our society at large.

CHAPTER 8
(pp. 23–4)

Focus on: Paula's reactions

GAUGE PAULA'S REACTIONS . . .

— What mixture of reactions does she seem to be experiencing? Start by choosing from among the following: shock, grief, anger, relief, a need to suppress strong feelings, confusion, fear, inquisitiveness, emptiness.

— For each reaction that you find, pinpoint how this is conveyed. To what extent does Doyle spell out her reactions, and to what extent does he hint at them?

GAUGE YOUR REACTIONS . . .
— The news that Paula eventually confronted Charlo and threw him out is closely followed by the surprising statements, 'I still loved him . . . I love him now' (p. 24). How do you react to these declarations? Do you feel angry at her abject victimhood or do you admire her enduring love? And how do you react to the claim that the minute she saw Charlo, Paula was 'nearly wanting him to be a bastard' (p. 24)? Do you find Paula's reactions to Charlo's death a true reflection of how a woman might really feel?

CHAPTER 9
(pp. 25–41)

Focus on: 'male' and 'female' memories

COMPARE AND ANALYSE . . .
— Look at Paula's account of her schooldays in this chapter and note the sorts of things she remembers. What were the aspects of primary school that she remembers loving? And what does she particularly remember about her secondary school that made her miserable? Now consider whether her memories can be called typically 'female'. To examine this question more fully, you might compare this chapter with pp. 180–7 of Doyle's novel *Paddy Clarke Ha Ha Ha*, which present Paddy's (recent) memories of his schooldays. Is there a noticeable gender divide in their perspectives on their schooldays?

Focus on: freedom and rules

EXAMINE . . .

— Paula's move from primary school meant the loss of a loving environment that encouraged the freedom of expression. What does it say about Paula's character that the happiest memories from her schooldays are of the secure, nurturing atmosphere at St Mary's? In what ways is the abusive, judgemental and rigid ethos of her secondary school completely wrong for her character? And what effects on the self-confident, happy, intelligent younger Paula are created by this change of schools? Finally, consider to what extent Paula's later acceptance of abusive behaviour that brutally invalidates her feelings was established at school.

Focus on: sex

UNPICK . . .

— Paula's developing attitudes to sex are polluted by the inflexible values that predominate, both at her school and in the wider society of early 1970s Dublin. Unpick the attitudes to sex that are expressed in this chapter and identify any instances of hypocrisy. Then look at how Doyle places Paula's comic account of 'My First Wank' in opposition to the hypocritical judgements she endures from others.

Focus on: language

LOOK FOR EXAMPLES . . .

— 'I didn't masturbate him: I wanked him' (p. 40). This is a nice distinction (in the original sense of 'a fine discrimination between two similar things'). Despite the vulgarity, Paula uses language with intelligent pleasure. Look for other examples where Paula uses language in an aware or a creative way.

CHAPTER 10
(pp. 42–3)

Focus on: then and now

COMPARE . . .

— Paula's comparison of herself as a teenager with herself as a thirty-nine-year-old woman focuses mainly on the degeneration of her body and the shrinking of her hopes. But not entirely. What aspects of the comparison suggest that in some ways she thinks her life has changed for the better?

CHAPTER 11
(pp. 43–5)

Focus on: Gerard

TRANSFORM . . .

— Transform the telephone conversation in this chapter into an interior monologue that explains Gerard's thoughts and feelings as he speaks to Paula.

CHAPTER 12
(pp. 45–54)

Focus on: sexist attitudes

EXAMINE AND ANALYSE . . .

— This chapter contains numerous references to the ideas of 'respect' and 'disrespect', especially towards women. Examine which behaviours brought respect to a man or to a woman when Paula was young, and which brought disrespect. The attitudes to women that Paula encounters are deeply sexist, but she seems to buy into them – perhaps because they are all she knows. Consider how her own language reflects sexist attitudes. For example, how has she used the word 'cunt' before now (see pp. 26 and 31)? Note how Paula falls in love with Charlo not because he treats her like an individual, but because being attached to him makes her feel less like nothing, and he therefore appears like a liberator from her low self-esteem. Consider the claim that some could say that Paula is a ripe candidate for abuse.

CHAPTER 13
(pp. 54–9)

Focus on: truth and stories

DISCUSS . . .
— Carmel challenges Paula's version of the past as 'rewriting history' (p. 56), but Paula insists that her stories about the past are true. Do we know who is right? We have already seen that Paula likes to make unpalatable experiences 'nice' by reinventing them in her imagination (p. 22); and her mention of Robert Redford (p. 58) recalls her tendency to confuse fact with fiction, especially if the fiction is more appealing than the fact. However, Paula clearly has a strong need to be able to trust as truthful her memories of her childhood as normal and happy. Discuss the claim that Paula's narrative is an attempt to create a story that reflects her inner truth if not the facts of her life.

CHAPTER 14
(pp. 60–4)

Focus on: mother and daughter

UNTANGLE . . .
— Untangle Paula's feelings about her daughter Nicola. How realistic is this portrait of a mother/daughter relationship?

Focus on: comedy and tragedy

EXTEND AND EXAMINE . . .
— 'It was a bit indecent, laughing at the way your husband had got himself killed' (p. 63). Notice how this statement distinguishes between 'decent' behaviour – whatever society dictates is acceptable – and the subversive power of humour to break through polite conventions. The way that Doyle's characters are able to find humour in even the grimmest and most unjust circumstances is one of their strengths. Consider the way we use humour in our lives to put human pain and insecurity into perspective – to rob them of their power to make us frightened. Making humour out of tragic events takes the sting out of the injustice and allows characters to stabilise their unstable worlds. You might want to extend your understanding of this aspect of comedy by listening to a tape of a professional comic, such as Billy Connolly, and noticing how often his humour makes subjects that are potentially painful, harmless. Or you might read Trevor Griffiths's play *Comedians* (1975), which presents a group of aspiring comedians who are trying to escape their working-class lives by breaking into the comedy circuit. The play examines the role of comedy: its power to hurt and its power to heal. 'Most comics feed prejudice and fear and blinkered vision, but the best ones, the best ones illuminate them, make them clearer to see, easier to deal with,' says Waters, the comics' teacher, in a way typical of the play's polemic method.

CHAPTER 15
(pp. 64–8)

Focus on: comic technique

IDENTIFY AND ANALYSE THE TECHNIQUE . . .
— This chapter is a wonderful example of Doyle's skill as a comic set-piece writer. He starts with a situation that is familiar to most readers – visiting a boyfriend's family for the first time, needing a pee desperately – and he develops the idea through stages so that we can enjoy, with a sense of anticipation that is then surpassed, the comic turns. Identify the way Doyle increases Paula's comic humiliation in carefully orchestrated stages. Note that this comic set piece is placed against dark underlying signs in Charlo's family background that explain his later brutality. How does this complicate our enjoyment of the comedy?

STUDY THE BALANCE . . .
— The slapstick comedy of this chapter ends with Paula considering the weight and trajectory of a pair of wet knickers, and regretting having to throw them away because 'A good pair they were too' (p. 68). Consider how Doyle balances the unlikely with the ordinary in his creation of comedy.

CHAPTER 16
(pp. 69–85)

Focus on: nostalgia

IDENTIFY . . .
— Paula's memories of her first loves and friendships have a nostalgic, innocent mood. Many of the themes of her adult life

are there in inchoate form (sexual desire, power, friendship), but her innocent understanding of these issues at eleven creates a nostalgic sense. Choose one page from this chapter and identify details that convey Paula's innocence at the age of eleven.

ANALYSE THE LANGUAGE . . .

— Examine further how this nostalgic mood is created by Doyle. You could approach this question by picking images that have an innocent feel, as above; or by focusing on the language. Go through this chapter and underline every occurrence of words that have a warm, nostalgic feel, like 'best friend', 'happy', 'trust', and so on. Once you have done this, ask yourself to what extent Doyle creates the mood of this chapter through the language he employs.

Focus on: dialogue

READ CLOSELY . . .

— Look closely at the dialogue on pp. 77–80, from '—Do you remember?' to '—I did it with Derek Kearns.' Doyle often portrays his characters through how they speak rather than through descriptions of what they look like or of how they act. As you read these pages, pay attention to the rhythms of the dialogue and to the language. What impressions do you have of Carmel from the way that she speaks?

SPOT THE PATTERN . . .

— Paula sees in Carmel someone who is 'Loving herself for hating herself' (p. 85), enjoying, in other words, her own self-hating drama. Paula, too, plays out her own self-hating drama: 'I was starting it again, nearly wishing him dead. To prove how hopeless I was, what a slut and an alco' (p. 84). Even her love for her children has a masochistic element: 'Big lumps of grief climbed up through me. I enjoyed it. The strength of it. My love being proved' (p. 84). Doyle understands well

the self-destructive dramas and self-regard of the unhappy, especially of alcoholics. Look for instances in which Paula seems
to be playing out a predetermined 'script' in her relations with
others. Do you find a pattern of behaviour emerging?

CHAPTER 17
(pp. 85–6)

Focus on: private vs public

NOTICE THE NARRATIVE TECHNIQUE . . .
— When Paula sees the news report of Charlo's murder, she
recognises the socks that the corpse is wearing: 'I'd bought them
for him' (p. 86). How does this short chapter set up a tension
between the public news coverage of Charlo's shooting and
Paula's private feelings about it, which are implied but not
stated? Notice how restrained her narrative is even when
discussing such personal events. In what ways does this restraint
increase the power of the narrative?

CHAPTER 18
(pp. 86–116)

Focus on: Paula's self-portrayal

ASSESS . . .
— This long chapter falls at the centre of the novel. Until
now, the reader has pieced together an impression of Paula's
life from a jigsaw of assorted clues. Now she tries to make a
deliberate, explicit and fairly comprehensive statement about
the facts of her life, filling in the gaps; but she keeps getting
sidetracked on to how she feels about things. Perhaps the real

significance of much of what she says in this chapter is what it reveals about her state of mind – her habit of cleaning up after others, both at work and at home, for instance; her love for her children; her loneliness and sexual frustration; her self-loathing because of her drinking. Assess what this chapter adds to our understanding of Paula.

Focus on: walk-on parts

EVALUATE . . .

— Doyle has said that the difference between a good film and a great film is in the quality of the walk-on parts, and that the same can be said of the novel. Look at the walk-on characters in this chapter and make a judgement about how well they are portrayed.

CHAPTER 19
(pp. 116–21)

Focus on: Paula's father

LOOK FOR SIMILARITIES . . .

— 'My father was a nice man but he could be very contrary and stubborn. He was being protective, I suppose; no one was good enough for his daughter' (p. 119). Do you share Paula's impressions of her father, or is she fooling herself? There are signs that her father has changed in middle age: 'He was different too. He'd become a bitter pill and a bully' (p. 120). Look for signs in this chapter that, as the older Paula says, her father and Charlo 'were very alike' (p. 121).

CHAPTER 20
(pp. 121–8)

Focus on: evil

ACCOUNT FOR . . .

— Paula uses the word 'evil' on p. 122 to describe Charlo's actions towards Mrs Fleming. This is the first time in the narrative that she has been morally judgmental of Charlo. She uses the word again on p. 216, when Paula is shaken to see Charlo's malice towards their daughter Nicola, an incident that predates the former. In both cases she makes the moral judgment only when Charlo threatens another person: in relation to herself, she is accepting of all of his behaviour. What in Paula's narrative so far accounts for this inability to stand up for her own rights?

Focus on: lies

IDENTIFY . . .

— 'The things we say. Sometimes they make no sense, sometimes they're just packed with lies. I'm grand. Don't mind me. *You fell.* It's okay, love' (p. 122). In what specific ways have we already seen that Paula's life is steeped in lies?

Focus on: reconstruction

RELATE THE CHAPTER TO THE WHOLE NOVEL . . .

— Paula reconstructs Charlo's actions at the Flemings' house from accounts she has read. This is therefore a story at three removes: an account based on several other accounts which were based on witness accounts of events. Paula is aware that there are parts of the story left unsaid: 'There were things that had happened in that house that I'd never know about. Because there was no evidence. There were no witnesses. No one and nothing' (p. 122). Consider how this chapter foregrounds the theme throughout the novel of the gap between the truth and stories about the truth.

NOTE THE TENSIONS . . .
— Paula's life has largely been an exercise in maintaining lies (see above). The emotional imperative behind her whole narrative is to reconstruct events so that she can finally make sense – which even now may not be the same as making truth – of them. Note the tensions in Paula's account of Charlo's actions. Why, for instance, does she say that 'It upset me that Charlo had done all this with someone I'd never known' (p. 126)? In what ways does her account betray that she both sees his actions as 'evil' and feels deeply attached to him, even jealous of him?

CHAPTER 21
(pp. 128–43)

Focus on: stories

TRACE THE IRONIES . . .
— Paula tells the story of the early, obsessive stages of her relationship with Charlo. Look at how she tells these stories. For instance, notice the number of emphatic, definitive statements that she makes early on in the chapter about how happy, how in love they were. Notice also her focus on photographs as hard evidence of what actually happened. Her story includes the other stories that she and Charlo told at the time about what they would do together, the places that they would visit – but never did. Notice how, as the chapter unfolds, the initial certainties start to sound less secure; the claims of bliss give way to the truth about her disappointment, even on the wedding night. In the end, Paula's story is deeply ironic: she married Charlo

to spite her bullying father, but ended up being trapped in a far more bullying and disempowering relationship. Examine how the ironies work in this chapter: how does Doyle convey, behind Paula's simplified stories, a sense of the compromised nature of human experience?

Focus on: photographs

COMPARE . . .

— This chapter emphasises photographs as reliable evidence of the past – an idea that goes to the heart of Paula's project, which is to make sense of the past from the evidence available to her. Consider photographs as evidence of the past. In one sense they offer incontrovertible truth; but in another they can be deceptive and open to interpretation, and to storytelling. To explore further the idea of photographs as unreliable evidence of the past, read Philip Larkin's poem 'Lines on a Young Lady's Photograph Album'. Compare Larkin's notions of inventing the past with Doyle's, in this novel.

CHAPTER 22
(pp. 143–7)

Focus on: healing

DISCERN . . .

— Why does Paula visit the Flemings' house? Notice the imagery of life, space and beauty that she sees there. She would rather imagine Mr Fleming than actually see him because 'It made more sense' (p. 147). One might ask to whom. Is this account another instance of Paula 'making it nice' (p. 22) in her imagination? Does her capacity to imagine a beauty greater than the reality merely constitute escapism, or is it genuinely healing?

CHAPTER 23
(pp. 147–56)

Focus on: honeymooning

ASSESS . . .

— Paula's memories of her honeymoon are of a happy, intimate and exciting time. We have come to recognise her capacity for seeing things as she would like to see them, however, rather than how they really were. Look carefully over this chapter and assess Charlo's behaviour on their honeymoon. Is it your impression that he was as much in love as she was? Are there any details which make you think that the happiness and intimacy Paula remembers might have been largely in her own mind, or do you have the impression that this was a mutually satisfying time for them? This account comes quite late in the narrative, after we know that their relationship became abusive. How does that knowledge affect our reading of Paula's account of their honeymoon?

CHAPTER 24
(pp. 156–62)

Focus on: evidence

CONSIDER . . .

— 'I wanted none of the answers that started to breathe in me; I smothered them. They were all horrible. They were all just savage and brutal. Nasty and sick. They mocked my marriage, my love; they mocked my whole life' (p. 158). Whereas Paula always found a way to accept Charlo's violence towards her as part of a loving relationship, she cannot see his violence towards a stranger as anything other than violence – and this difficult fact forces her to reappraise her view of Charlo. Consider the ways in which this chapter develops the theme of evidence in the novel.

CHAPTER 25
(pp. 162–75)

Focus on: contrasting perspectives

COMPARE . . .

— The opening paragraphs on pp. 162–4 repeat a scene portrayed in Chapter 3 (p. 5), but this second account is different in significant ways. It includes some commentary by Paula that was missing from the earlier one. It also explains what happened – 'the fact that he'd hit me, plain and simple' (p. 163) – in unequivocal, explicit terms, whereas before Charlo's violence was left implied. Compare the two accounts. What does the comparison suggest about how far Paula is succeeding in facing up to her past, in looking at it clearly and being able to say the truth?

— Similarly, the short scene on p. 164 repeats and develops that in Chapter 7 (p. 23). What has been added? What is the effect of the nurse's presence, for instance? If she has seen Paula before, why doesn't she ask her about the multiple injuries? What do the details that she was 'nice' and 'her boyfriend was waiting' imply about her reasons for ignoring them? And what effect is created by including Paula's inner monologue, 'Ask me. Ask me. Ask me'?

Focus on: contrasting narratives

TELL THE STORY . . .

— Telling stories about our lives is one way in which we make sense of them. However, Paula is struggling to make sense of her experiences, and in this chapter she tells several different stories that contradict each other. Look at these statements:

- 'We were very, very happy' (p. 167).
- 'I was always tired; I remember that much' (p. 169).
- 'I could have avoided it' (p. 169).
- 'That fist was always coming towards me . . . It had nothing to do with me' (pp. 169–70).
- 'I was to blame' (p. 171).
- 'I'm innocent' (p. 171).

— Write your own account of why their marriage went wrong, based on your reading of the novel so far but especially on this chapter. Make clear who was to blame, in your opinion, and why. Also make clear whether or not Charlo loves Paula. Restrict yourself to three hundred words.

COMPARE . . .

— Doyle has said he admires Dorothy Allison's novel *Bastard Out of Carolina* (1992), the tale of a young girl who is physically and – eventually – sexually abused by her stepfather. This novel gives a vivid account of the feelings of guilt, self-blame and self-hatred of victims of abuse. Compare the ways that the two novels treat this theme. Otherwise, you might like to see if you can find the 1996 television film of that novel directed by Anjelica Huston.

CHAPTER 26
(pp. 175–203)

Focus on: truth-telling

CONSIDER AND APPLY . . .

— This chapter gives the brutal truth of Paula's suffering at Charlo's hands for seventeen miserable years of marriage. We now see a new portrait of Paula, the view of herself that she could not bear to confront before. The style changes, indicating a growing ability in Paula to see her own experiences for what they really were. Consider the following ten claims:

- This is the first point in the narrative at which Paula has been able to tell the full truth.
- It therefore represents – for her – a victory, namely the ability to speak up for herself without being asked.
- In it, she identifies her own low self-esteem as the source of her problems as much as the result of them.
- Her perspective is frequently presented as skewed, distorted, and she now sees this.
- She and Charlo seemed to inhabit an alternative reality dominated by unspoken rules that were insane.
- The chorus of Leanne's voice pleading 'Don't hit my mammy!' is like a touchstone to normal sanity.
- Paula now understands the full cruelty of the way that Charlo enjoyed his control over her and that he played with it.
- Paula recognises that she cannot transform her memories into a happy story.
- For a woman who has been scripted in living with lies, the ability to tell the truth and to see it clearly is a major step towards sanity.
- Therefore, this chapter represents more than a revelation

of the suffering she has undergone: it also represents a step in healing that suffering.

— To what extent do these claims illuminate what Doyle is doing in this chapter? Would you change or delete any of them, or add any claims of your own?

Focus on: the title

RELATE . . .
— 'I walked into the door' (p. 181). We see that Paula tells this lie because she feels frightened of further beatings. Charlo responds by patronising her and making her to blame. By telling the required lie, she has confirmed his control over her and given the cue for further humiliation. Now consider the fact that the novel takes its title from this lie. To what extent does the title foreground Paula's compliance in her abuse as a central aspect of it?

Focus on: being and not-being

ANALYSE THE LANGUAGE . . .
— Note how many phrases Paula uses on pp. 182–9 that are suggestive of non-existence. Her identity is almost extinguished. What does her language reveal about her state of mind? In what ways does this recall her mother? Look back at p. 120 and interpret her mother's state of mind. Is she, too, a person without an identity? Now consider why Charlo sets about to rob Paula of her sense of self. She becomes dependent on him and unable to leave. How else does it serve his purposes?

Focus on: complicity

RELATE . . .
'They didn't wink at each other because they didn't have to'

(p. 190). 'He was speaking on my behalf, for us both. His shock was mine, his opinions. I was always like that when Charlo was talking. I was happy listening to him' (p. 198). Look at the context of each of these quotations. Relate them to what the novel as a whole is saying about why decent people let themselves be complicit in obscene things.

Focus on: cruelty

INTERPRET . . .
— Look over the account of Charlo's cruelty to Paula in this chapter. She finds it incomprehensible. Can you explain it? Try interpreting his cruelty in terms of the following ideas, and see which seems to explain his behaviour best: power, anger, sadism, confusion, contempt, evil.

Focus on: the lost child

CONSIDER . . .
— Paula has hinted several times that she lost a child as a result of Charlo's violence (see pp. 177–8). Now she explains how, in a bleak little paragraph at the end of this chapter, on p. 203. 'I never saw her. Her name is Sally,' she says. Consider why Paula refers to Sally in the present tense, as if she is still alive. To what extent is Paula also a lost child, denied her life by Charlo's violence? Does she identify with her child?

CHAPTER 27
(pp. 203–6)

Focus on: mothering

READ CAREFULLY . . .
— Being a mother saves Paula from total self-extinction,

because her children depend on her. She may not care enough about herself or have enough strength to stand up for herself, but she has a strong instinct to protect and give hope to her children. How exactly does this chapter emphasise her strong love for her children?

CHAPTER 28
(pp. 206–14)

Focus on: imprisonment

REFLECT . . .

— Read pp. 206–10 and think about why it is that Paula feels unable to leave the house. Create a list of reasons why it would be better for her to go. Include in your list those things that you consider to be among the best that life has to offer. Why does she have no hope? What does it say about her view of herself and of life that she cannot bring herself to leave? How important a factor is her financial dependence on Charlo? To what extent is Paula's imprisonment a reality and to what extent does her prison really exist inside her head?

Focus on: metaphor

ANALYSE THE LANGUAGE . . .

— 'I couldn't go through the door, so I fucked him through it instead' (p. 214). What does Paula mean by 'fucked' here? Unlike the standard idiom 'No fuckin' way' a few lines above, this is an unusual use of the word. It seems to equate sex with violence, rejection and hatred. Does this metaphor relate to her attitudes to sex during the novel?

CHAPTER 29
(pp. 214–25)

Focus on: John Paul

CREATE . . .

— In this chapter we get a brief insight into John Paul's life. What have we been told about him so far in the novel? Is he also a victim? His story remains on the margins, largely untold. Tell it for him by writing a three-hundred-word summary of his life, from his point of view and in his voice. Then consider what effects are created by his silence in the novel.

Focus on: revenge

REVIEW . . .

— Paula has earlier described the moment of hitting Charlo as 'My finest hour. I was there. I was something. I loved' (p. 213). In what ways has the novel prepared us to see her violence in Chapter 29 as her finest hour?

Focus on: religion

CONSIDER THE CLAIM . . .

— This chapter contains several indirect religious allusions: to the 'evil' in Charlo; to John Paul's name, which was that of the Pope at the time of publication; the imprecations 'Jesus!' and 'hell!'. But none of these are actually about religion. Consider the claim that the Church's influence is notable by its absence in Paula's life.

CHAPTER 30
(p. 225)

Focus on: balanced perspectives

DISCERN THE AUTHORIAL TECHNIQUE . . .

— This chapter re-presents a scene that was presented in Chapter 17 on pp. 85–6. We now know far more about Charlo than we did when we read the earlier chapter, and in particular about what a monster he was. So our instinct is to think he got what he deserved. But notice how Paula's point of view is complicated by her residual love and generosity towards him. Her narrative on p. 225 depicts him as a victim, lost and alone, far from home. Note how often Doyle balances our perspective, forcing the reader continually to adjust his or her perspective, while maintaining a dispassionate distance himself.

CHAPTER 31
(p. 226)

Focus on: goodness

DISCUSS . . .

— 'I'd done something good' (p. 226). What is goodness ultimately equated with in this novel?

Looking over the whole novel

QUESTIONS FOR DISCUSSION OR ESSAYS

1. 'Doyle never judges his characters, but forgives them everything.' To what extent is this claim true of the characters in *The Woman Who Walked Into Doors*?

2. 'Doyle manages to create humour without ever undermining the seriousness of the issues his characters face.' Have you found this to be true of his portrayal of wife abuse and alcoholism in *The Woman Who Walked Into Doors*?

3. How important is Paula's relationship with her father in establishing the pattern of her later relationship with Charlo, do you think?

4. Examine the portrayal of 'family' in *The Woman Who Walked Into Doors*.

5. Consider the theme of power and powerlessness in *The Woman Who Walked Into Doors*.

6. Discuss the presentation of the relationship of truth to memory in *The Woman Who Walked Into Doors*.

7. Consider how *The Woman Who Walked Into Doors* layers dreams with reality and romance with violence.'

8. Discuss notions of truth and storytelling as they are presented in the novel.

9. What does *The Woman Who Walked Into Doors* have to say about the role of women in a patriarchal society?

10. 'Paula's main problem is not that Charlo hates her, but that she hates herself.' Discuss.

11. 'Paula is not a victim: throughout, she is a survivor.' Discuss.

12. Examine the ways that the novel presents physical and emotional violence.

13. How convincingly does Doyle create the consciousness of an abused and alcoholic woman in *The Woman Who Walked Into Doors*?

14. Consider the ways in which Doyle uses dialogue to create character.

15. Discuss Doyle's use of narrative voice in the creation of Paula Spencer's character in *The Woman Who Walked Into Doors*.

16. How hopeful do you find the ending of *The Woman Who Walked Into Doors*?

Contexts, comparisons and complementary readings

THE WOMAN WHO WALKED INTO DOORS

These sections suggest contextual and comparative ways of reading these works by Doyle. You can put your reading in a social, historical or literary context. You can make comparisons – again, social, literary or historical – with other texts or art works. Or you can choose complementary works (of whatever kind) – that is, art works, literary works, social reportage or facts which in some way illuminate the text by sidelights or interventions which you can make into a telling framework. Some of the suggested contexts are directly connected to the book, in that they will give you precise literary or social frames in which to situate the novel. In turn, these are either related to the period within which the novel is set, or to the time – now – when you are reading it. Some of these examples are designed to suggest books or other texts that may make useful sources for comparison (or for complementary purposes) when you are reading *The Woman Who Walked Into Doors*. Again, they may be related to literary or critical themes, or they may be relevant to social and cultural themes current 'then' or 'now'.

Focus on: 'realism'

READ AND APPLY . . .

— Doyle has said that his job as a novelist is 'to describe things and people as they really are'. Look up 'realism' in the Glossary. 'The realist is deliberately selective in material and prefers the average, the commonplace and the everyday over the rarer aspects of the social scene. The characters, therefore, are usually of the middle class or (less frequently) the working class – people without exceptional endowments, who live through ordinary experiences of childhood, adolescence, love, marriage, parenthood, infidelity, and death; who find life rather dull and often unhappy, though it may be brightened by touches of beauty and joy' (M. H. Abrams). According to which of these criteria can *The Woman Who Walked Into Doors* be called a realist novel?

Focus on: the comic perspective

DISCRIMINATE . . .

— Comedy and humour do not mean quite the same thing when applied to literature. Look them up in the Glossary. Doyle's novels present some of the bleaker aspects of life, and his plots show characters meeting the challenges of their lives in a way that is typical of comedy. They are also able to find humour in even the grimmest and most unjust circumstances. His novels are therefore both comic and humorous. However, Doyle's social vision has become steadily darker over the years, so that the humour and optimism of his first two works has gradually become eclipsed by a sense of the overwhelming difficulties in the lives of his characters. Although there is some hope at the end of each novel, the comic aspects of Doyle's work have become less pronounced, and his humour has become grimmer. Look at Caramine White's comments on this topic in the Selected Extracts section on pages 212–3.

Focus on: religion

EXAMINE . . .
— Like most of Doyle's characters, Paula and Charlo are nominally Roman Catholic, but the Church and its sacraments do not figure importantly in their lives, nor does religious faith help Paula meet the difficulties that life presents her. Of the only priest who visits her after her traumatic marriage, Paula says, 'it wasn't my tea he was after, or my biscuits. It isn't only the bishops who like to get their exercise' (p. 90). Doyle is critical of the influence of Catholicism in Ireland, which he describes as 'Catholicism without the colour', and does not regret the fact that the influence of the Church on the State has waned in recent years. Examine what Doyle has said about religion in interviews (see pages 212–3 for examples).

Focus on: politics

RESEARCH . . .
— Doyle describes himself as socially committed and politically engaged. Most of his writing touches on issues of social politics (class struggles, divorce, domestic violence), but he decries political correctness as anathema to good writing, especially to satire. The television series *The Family* was his most overtly political work, and he admits to having enjoyed the outrage it caused for its bleak presentation of family life. His work is rarely overtly political, however. His own family back-

ground was largely Republican, and his own political instincts are socialist, but he does not belong to a political party and he has repeatedly said that fiction should not be a vehicle for the novelist to preach politics. Find out about Doyle's political engagement, using the inteview and the Selected extracts from critical writings in this guide as a starting point.

Focus on: domestic violence

RESEARCH AND DISCUSS . . .
— Most married couples have disagreements; luckily, only a small minority resort to physical violence. How widespread is the problem of domestic violence? Consider and discuss the following statistics published by Women's Aid in Dublin in 2002:

● 'Almost one in five women have experienced domestic violence by a current or former intimate partner or boyfriend.'
● 'Children are often present when violence is taking place.'
● 'Violence often occurs during pregnancy, and actual or threatened miscarriage can occur.'
● 'Just under 50% of men who abuse children also abuse women.'
— Now consider these statistics from the United States:

● 'Over two-thirds of violent victimizations against women were committed by someone known to them: Approximately 28% were intimates such as husbands or boyfriends. Almost 6 times as many women victimized by intimates (18%) as those victimized by strangers (3%) did not report their violent victimization to police because they feared reprisal from the offender.' (Ronet Bachman, PhD, US

Department of Justice Bureau of Justice Statistics, 'Violence Against Women: A National Crime Victimization Survey Report', January 1994, p. 1)

- 'Battered women seek medical attention for injuries sustained as a consequence of domestic violence significantly more often after separation than during cohabitation; about 75% of the visits to emergency rooms by battered women occur after separation.' (Stark and Flitcraft, 1988)

- 'There are 1,500 shelters for battered women in the United States. There are 3,800 animal shelters.' (Schneider, 1990)

- 'Violence is the reason stated for divorce in 22% of middle-class marriages.' (EAP Digest, November/December 1991)

RESEARCH AND COMPARE . . .

— Although we have now invented the term 'domestic violence' to describe the kinds of abuse (usually of women and children, and usually by men) that goes on in homes, the thing itself has actually been a commonplace across the centuries. In the West, up until the nineteenth century, women were regarded by society as a whole as a husband's chattel, to do with as he liked, and if that included knocking out her teeth then there was nothing to be done about it. Books from earlier periods that deal with this subject – albeit indirectly – might include Samuel Richardson's *Clarissa* (1748–9) where Lovelace abducts and, in the end, rapes Clarissa Harlowe; Charles Dickens's *Oliver Twist* (1837–8) where Bill Sikes regularly beats, and eventually murders, his girlfriend Nancy; Emily Brontë's *Wuthering Heights* (1847) where Heathcliff's domestic abuse is obliquely described. Early plays on the same subject might include Shakespeare's *The Taming of the Shrew* (*c.* 1592) and Middleton and Rowley's *The Changeling* (*c.* 1622). More recent books that feature kinds of abuse – physical and mental – might include Charlotte Perkins Gilman's *The Yellow Wallpaper* (1892), F. Scott Fitzgerald's *Tender is the Night* (1934) or William Styron's *Sophie's*

Choice (1976). One important text that – like *The Woman Who Walked Into Doors* – deals with the issue from the woman's point of view is Alice Walker's *The Color Purple* (1983). Another, from the child's point of view, is Dorothy Allison's *Bastard Out of Carolina* (1992).

— Otherwise, you might have come across a song on the subject: Tracy Chapman's 'Behind the Wall' from her 1989 album *Tracy Chapman*.

— Choose any one of these texts and compare the treatment of the subject with that offered in Doyle's novel.

Focus on: unofficial narratives

COMPARE . . .

— Explore the idea of 'the unofficial narrative'. *The Woman Who Walked Into Doors* gives a voice to a character who has no voice, who is ignored, invalidated and marginalised. Beneath her story is a universal story of countless other invisible women whose lives go untold. Seen in these terms, the novel can be compared with two other works that give the unofficial narratives for marginalised and voiceless groups of black women in the United States, Toni Morrison's *Beloved* (1987) and Alice Walker's *The Color Purple* (1983). This is what Morrison has said on this topic, when talking about the cultural narrative about slavery in the United States:

> I want to scour the official history for the alternate
> history that exists, sometimes parallel to it, more
> often underneath it. It gleams through the official
> story in curious ways – a shot here, a facet there –
> and it's the kind of thing you want to pursue, and
> when you cannot find all of the data, you have to

imagine it. But I don't want the story, the alternate, or underneath or repressed story, told in a manner that duplicates the official narrative. I want the speakers, the characters, to assume whatever format they wish. Sometimes it's their thoughts, sometimes it's a fugue, sometimes it's just incredible kinds of silence.

Vintage Living Texts: Toni Morrison (2003).

— Walker's subject is closer to Doyle's in several key ways: it is the secret confession of a young woman who is the victim of domestic violence, who is struggling to achieve a sense of who she is. Compare the ways in which either of these novels presents the idea of the unofficial narrative with *The Woman Who Walked Into Doors*.

Focus on: stage adaptation

ANALYSE THE LANGUAGE . . .

— *The Woman Who Walked Into Doors* has been adapted for the stage by writer/director Joe O'Byrne, and received its first staging at the Helix in Dublin in May 2003, with Brian F. O'Byrne as Charlo and Hilda Fay as Paula. Read the following excerpts from a review by Harvey O'Brien and consider how the critic highlights the challenges posed by staging this novel:

The Woman Who Walked Into Doors is an adult pantomime, a cautionary tale writ large through characters defined by extravagant gesture, elaborate costume, and direct address to the audience. The play employs stylized exaggeration which invites laughter and terror, veering from the song-and-dance farce of a Dublin disco in the 1970s (complete with afro-wearing dudes and glam rock tunes) to the balletic, slow-motion depiction of acts of domestic violence . . . It takes almost an hour before the first act of domestic violence, portrayed with a sudden flash of light and a dreamlike aftermath which is then repeated as Paula tries to make sense of what has just happened . . . Only once does the domestic violence happen in 'real time', and it is a genuinely shocking moment. The rest of the time Charlo's cruelty is seen and shown as a kind of performance. O'Byrne stands away from Fay, punching the air. Interlocking and overlapping live and recorded narration describes the catalogue of injuries inflicted. Even the cathartic climax where Paula hit Charlo with a frying pan employs stylized action which stops short of literal depiction.

O'Byrne maintains his jutting-elbowed stance, jerky neck movements, and monosyllabic conversation throughout the piece, usually to peals of laughter from the appreciative crowd. It is little wonder that, by the end, the actor received a chorus of good-natured 'boos' followed by an indulgent round of laughter and applause. Panto it is, then. Fay, for her part, captures the complexity of her character's feelings and gives the play a strong physical and vocal centre. Unable and/or unwilling to leave her husband and the father of her children, Paula is torn by feelings of love and respect in tandem with fear and (self) hatred. Fay does a good job of representing the mixture of strength and weakness which defines her character and is remark-able in the scenes where she is thrown around the set like a rag doll.

Focus on: the opera

FIND OUT ABOUT . . .

— *The Woman Who Walked Into Doors – The Opera,* with music by the Belgian jazz composer Kris Defoort, was first performed in Antwerp in 2001. In October 2003, it was presented by the Dublin Theatre Festival and Opera Ireland at the Gaity Theatre in Dublin.

— In this adaptation the part of Paula was performed by two people: the actress Jacqueline Blom and the singer Claron McFadden. Onstage throughout there was also a giant video screen playing out a counterpoint to the music and the libretto. Find out what you can about this production.

MAKE UP YOUR OWN . . .

— What do you think of a novel like *The Woman Who Walked Into Doors* being made into an opera? Why might the subject matter make it a good choice for such treatment? Why might the style of the novel make it ripe for adaptation? Remember that there has also been a stage adaptation.

— If you decided to make *The Woman Who Walked Into Doors* into a play, or an opera, or a film, how would you go about it? What technical devices would you use? How would you set out the chronology? (Doyle says something about this in the interview on pages 22–4.) How would you convey Paula's younger self and her older self? How would your adaptation end? Sketch yourself a plan of your own production.

VINTAGE
LIVING
TEXTS

Reference

Selected extracts from critical writings

These brief extracts from critical articles on Doyle's work are designed to be used to suggest angles on the texts that may be relevant to their themes, their settings, their literary methods, their historical contexts, or to indicate their relevance to issues, questions or problems today.

Sometimes one critic's opinion will be entirely contradicted by another's. You might use these passages to ask yourself whether or not you agree with the writers' assessments. Or else you might take phrases from these articles to use for framing questions – for discussion, or for essays – about the texts.

None of these critical opinions are the last word. They are simply contributions to a cultural debate. As such, they should be approached with intellectual interest and intelligent assessment. But in the end, it is your own reading of a text that really counts.

Denis Donoghue
From 'Another Country' in *The New York Review of Books*,
Vol. 41, no. 3 (3 February 1994)
On the setting and frame for Barrytown

The most striking features of Barrytown in the years
denoted by *The Commitments, The Snapper* and *The
Van* are these: decline in the influence of the
Catholic Church on working-class families; general
indifference to modern Ireland and to the history of
dissent and revolt from which the country slowly
emerged; and incessant use of what my mother
called bad language.

Fintan O'Toole
From 'Working-Class Dublin on Screen: The Roddy Doyle
Films' in *Cinéaste*, Vol. 24, nos 2–3 (1999)
On Irishness and authenticity

In 1999 *Cinéaste* held a film symposium in New York
where, among other things, they asked eminent filmmakers a number of questions about the 'new' Irish
film industry including: '1. Is it possible . . . to make
culturally 'authentic' Irish films that can succeed
financially in a global marketplace? 2. Which of the
clichés or stereotypes perpetuated in previous screen
portrayals of Ireland and the Irish, films produced
predominantly by American and British filmmakers,
do you consider most annoying or objectionable? 3.
What sort of films should Irish filmmakers be
producing?'
Roddy Doyle's answers to these questions were:
'1. Yes, although we could spend the rest of our

lives discussing what we mean by 'authentic' and 'Irish' and what happens when we put the two words together. There are those who would maintain that you cannot be Irish and speak English, and there are those who would insist that your cannot dance authentically and lift your hands above your waist, and there are those who would say that the *The Commitments* isn't an Irish film. It's a small country, as are the minds of some of our cultural guardians.

'2. The section of your question referring to "films produced predominantly by American and British filmmakers" annoys me. Would you ask American filmmakers which clichés and stereotypes in *Paris, Texas, Some Like It Hot, Thelma and Louise, Interview with a Vampire* – all American films made by Europeans – annoy them? Some of the best Irish films of the last ten years, and a lot of the worst, have been made by people who don't happen to be Irish. And some of the best Irish films, and a lot of the worst, have been made by people who do happen to be Irish.

'3. Good ones.'

Lorraine Piroux
From '"I'm Black an' I'm Proud": Re-inventing Irishness in Roddy Doyle's *The Commitments*' in *College Literature*, Vol. 25, no. 2 (Spring 1988)
On Irishness and difference

In the work of Roddy Doyle . . . there are no explicit references to an Irish national consciousness or an Irish identity of the kind that had informed Irish writing since the early years of the independence movement. Doyle's first novel *The Commitments* suggests on the contrary that Irish identity does not exist in and of itself but springs from variegated possibilities of transnational solidarity with the disenfranchised. Being Irish, his young protagonists contend, is synonymous with being Black because oppression is Black. Thus Irishness is never fully realised in Doyle's writing, nor is it in the slightest way represented in metaphorical, symbolic or even descriptive narratives. It is in fact the very notion of identity, I argue, that Doyle's minimalist writing deconstructs when he uproots Irishness from those historical and narrative conventions which had served the interest of Irish nationalism earlier in the century. Irishness in *The Commitments* is no longer a matter of definition or semantics since Doyle does not ask what it means to be Irish. Rather, identity manifests itself in the sheer intensity of the dialogues, the slang and the lyrics of blues and soul music.

Caramine White
From *Reading Roddy Doyle* (Syracuse University Press, New York, 2001)
On tragedy, comedy and struggle as a concept

Doyle abandoned the Barrytown trilogy – with all its broad humour, wisecracking characters, and profanity-laced dialogue – in order to grow as an artist. Despite these novels' strengths and appeal, ultimately they are not as complex as his next two novels. Although Doyle grounds all of his novels in social realism, the world of the trilogy (particularly

the first two novels) is a world of comic resolution;
Doyle uses comedy to smooth over many uncomfort-
able, jagged edges. For instance, the Commitments'
demise is almost forgotten in the subsequent riotous
comedic scenes, and Sharon's rape in *The Snapper*
similarly gets glossed over, her final laughter
demonstrating both her own well-being and the
well-being of her baby. In *The Van*, Doyle's
transitional work, the same humour is present but
the conclusion is not smoothed over: Jimmy and
Bimbo do not repair their close friendship, an
ending that stuns the reader who anticipates a happy
reconciliation. Doyle's next two novels depict long-
term conflict and hardship: despite Paddy Clarke's
magical rituals and charm, his parents' separation is
far from cheering; in *The Woman Who Walked Into
Doors*, Paula struggles daily to overcome her
problems, and even humour – although healing –
cannot eliminate her cravings for alcohol. In these
two novels, Doyle's characters must struggle with
difficult problems, resulting in more ambitious, more
complex works that do not provide any easy
solutions for realistically painful problems.

Roy Foster
From *A Star Called Henry*, review in the *Guardian*,
August 1999
On destiny, realism and magic, and literary antecedents

Doyle [in *A Star Called Henry*] . . . avoids creaky
verismo by using a carefully gauged admixture of
magic-realist techniques. Henry's status as a child of
his century owes something to Rushdie's *Midnight's*

Children, his supernormal abilities to Grass's *The Tin Drum*, his take on history to Carter's *Wise Children*. This is august company, but *A Star Called Henry* holds its own with them, as with the historical novel it most resembles: John Barth's *The Sot-Weed Factor*. The protagonist's ruthlessness is mixed with an innocence that protects as well as condemns him. 'History' is a joke and a jade, and mysterious characters come and go such as Henry's teacher and lover Miss O'Shea, and the Brechtian boss figure, Alfie Gandon, with whom the revolution, and the novel, begins and ends.

Through it all runs a sense of destiny, symbolised, as in *Finnegans Wake*, by the water that runs through Dublin. Henry, like his father, can divine water: he can slip through a manhole cover, leaving only a 'clang in the air', and swim through sewersludge and underground rivers to safety. Doyle uses tricks like this to the limit of their effectiveness. For the rest, as in his other books, the dialogue does the work, with an unforced brilliance that conceals the art behind it.

Colm Tóibín
From 'New Ways to Kill Your Father', in the *New York Review of Books*, Vol. 50, no. 10 (12 June 2003)
On the ordinariness of bliss

He is concerned to dramatize [in *Rory and Ita*] a number of subjects uncommon in Irish writing, including his own previous work – niceness, decency, love, harmony, gentleness, kindness, prosperity, gentility. Thus cooking and going to work in the morning, acquiring a first refrigerator or a first washing machine, the buying of a dress or suit, the going to a dance or visiting friends, in all their mundane detail, are central events in the book, are allowed the space normally reserved for bitterness and violence in Irish books. This move into sweetness may arise partly from the genuine affection that Doyle feels for his parents, but it also comes from the sort of politics that has been central to his work from the beginning.

Glossary of literary terms

Allusion A conscious reference to another text, work of art, idea or historical fact which is designed to have some relevance to the situations described and which an informed reader will usually spot (since most allusions rely for their effect on the reader understanding them).

Bathos The effect created, intentionally or not, when a passage that attempts to be elevated in tone instead drops into the trivial or the ridiculous, or when an elevated style is combined with everyday subjects. It can also describe the effect created when an author employs trite sentimentality to manipulate a reader's sympathies.

Chronology A list of events as they take place in the order of real time.

Cliché Though *clichés* have never been the flavour of the month, we will leave no stone unturned until we have got the bit between our teeth and washed them right out of our hair. A *cliché* is an expression or an idea that is so well worn that it no longer has a cutting edge.

Comedy 'Comedy' denotes a literary form which usually presents a sympathetic protagonist meeting and overcoming difficulties of an ordinary kind, familiar to the reader or audience, and which therefore asserts a general human capacity for endurance and survival.

217

Episode A passage in a story that tells the events at one particular scene or moment. Characters may look forward to it, or recall it, so the reader might revisit that 'episode' several times.

Farce A type of comedy that uses exaggerated characters in ludicrous situations, usually involving physical humour, e.g. Charlie Chaplin comedies.

Foreground To bring to the front, to emphasise.

Grotesque In literature, the ridiculous, the freakish and the unnatural, often used for satirical or comic effect.

Humour An element of comedy, but more specifically a reaction to a recognition of an incongruity that gives way to laughter: it is a way of acknowledging the injustices of life and therefore of controlling our awareness of the dangers that life holds.

Interior monologue A narrative technique used when a character speaks their own thoughts to themselves in their own head. Hamlet's 'To be or not to be' speech is a monologue and would be an interior monologue if it took place in a novel.

Juxtapose To place side by side, for effect.

Metaphor Any figure of speech by which one thing is explained or described by relating it to some other thing. For instance, 'the whirligig of time', in which 'whirligig' is the image designed to tell us something about the nature of time – i.e. it brings everything back round again.

Nostalgia The sentimental hankering after what is past and irrecoverable.

Pathos The effect of evoking feelings of pity or sympathetic sorrow in a reader or audience.

Realism 'Realism' is a mode of writing fiction that sets out to give the illusion that it reflects real life as the ordinary reader might see it. It is an illusion in the sense that this is a carefully studied effect, created by careful choice of subject matter, detail and language.

Register The language, style and vocabulary appropriate to a particular subject.

Set piece A passage or episode that is set aside from the action in general so that it has a status of its own.

Situation Comedy A form of comedy that presents stock situations and easily recognisable character types, and often involves elements of farce. A common type of television comedy, e.g. 'Fawlty Towers' and 'Absolutely Fabulous'.

Slapstick Knockabout comedy, including boisterous and clownish physical buffoonery.

Stream of consciousness A narrative technique which sets out to mimic the many thoughts, feelings and impressions that pass through the mind. James Joyce used the technique in the opening of *A Portrait of the Artist as a Young Man* (1916) and developed it to its limits in *Ulysses* (1922).

Tragedy A serious play (or literary work) showing the downfall of some important character or characters. Sometimes the key to these events is a 'tragic flaw' in the character of the protagonist themselves. In ancient Greek tradition, it is the highest form of dramatic and literary art.

Typography The style, arrangement or appearance of the types.

Biographical outline

1958 8 May: Roddy Doyle born in Kilbarrack, a suburb of Dublin.

1976–80 Attended University College Dublin. BA in Geography and English, then diploma in Education.

1980 Begins teaching English and Geography at Greendale Community School, Kilbarrack.

1986 With John Sutton, founded King Farouk Publishing.

1987 *The Commitments* published by King Farouk.
Brownbread produced at the SFX Theatre, Dublin.

1988 *The Commitments* published in England by Heinemann.

1990 *The Snapper* published by Secker & Warburg.

1991 *The Van* published. Film of *The Commitments* released.

1993 *Paddy Clarke Ha Ha Ha* published. Won the Booker Prize for *Paddy Clarke Ha Ha Ha*. Film of *The Snapper* released. Became a full-time writer.

1994 *The Family* broadcast.

1996 *The Woman Who Walked Into Doors* published. Film of *The Van* released.

1999 *A Star Called Henry* published.

2002 *Rory and Ita* published.

Select bibliography

WORKS BY RODDY DOYLE

The Commitments (King Farouk, Dublin, 1987; Heinemann, London, 1988; Vintage, London, 1998)

The Snapper (Secker & Warburg, London, 1990; Vintage, 1998)

The Van (Secker & Warburg, 1991; Vintage, 1998).

Brownbread and *War* (Secker & Warburg, 1992)

Paddy Clarke Ha Ha Ha (Secker & Warburg, 1993; Vintage, 1998)

The Woman Who Walked Into Doors (Jonathan Cape, London, 1996; Vintage, 1998)

A Star Called Henry (Jonathan Cape, 1999; Vintage, 2000)

Rory and Ita (Jonathan Cape, 2002; Vintage, 2003)

INTERVIEWS

Roddy Doyle interviewed by Nuala O'Faolain, in *Bookliners*, RTE, Dublin (27 May 1993).

'Something of a Hero: An Interview with Roddy Doyle', in the *Literary Review* (Summer 1999).

Roddy Doyle interviewed by Dave Weich, in Powells Interviews (4 October, 1999), at *www.powells.com*

Roddy Doyle interviewed by Charles Taylor, in The Salon Interview (28 October, 1999), at *www.salon.com*

CRITICISM

Tim Adams, 'Hot Roddy', in the *Observer* (7 April 1996).

Keith M. Booker, 'Late Capitalism Comes to Dublin: Popular Culture in the Novels of Roddy Doyle', in *Ariel*, Vol. 28, part 3 (July 1997), pp. 27–45.

Nick Bradshaw, 'Doyle's Dubliners', in *Detail* (February 1994), pp. 128–30.

Terence Brown, *Ireland: A Social and Cultural History, 1922–1985* (Fontana Press, London, 1985).

Gabriel Byrne, John Carney, Roddy Doyle, Clare Duignanet *et al.*, 'Irish Cinema at the Crossroads: A Filmmaker's Symposium', in *Cinéaste* (1999). Useful quotes on the books as well as on the films.

Lawrence Christon, 'Doyle Talks the Talk', in *Los Angeles Times* (23 March 1994).

Brian Cossgrove, 'Roddy Doyle's Backward Look: Tradition and Modernity in *Paddy Clarke Ha Ha Ha*', in *Studies: An Irish Quarterly Review*, Vol. 85 (Autumn, 1996), pp. 231–42.

Seamus Deane, *Nationalism, Colonialism and Literature* (University of Minnesota Press, Minneapolis, 1990).

Denis Donoghue, 'Another Country', in *New York Review of Books*, Vol. 41, no. 3 (3 February 1994), pp. 3–6. A thoughtful and intelligent account of Doyle's style and content.

Roy Foster, *Modern Ireland, 1600–1972* (Penguin Press, New York, 1988).

Roy Foster, 'Roddy and the ragged-trousered revolutionary', in the *Guardian* (August 1999).

Dermot McCarthy, *Roddy Doyle: Raining on the Parade* (The Liffey Press, 2003). An up-to-date account of Doyle's work in relation to the complicated contemporary Irish scene. Especially good on the language and the setting of the novels.

Gerry McGuinness, *The Commitments: The Story of How and Where This Film Was Made in Ireland* (GLI, Dublin, 1996).

Daphne Merkin, 'The Critics: Roddy Doyle and Ron Hansen

take on history', in *The New Yorker* (4 October 1999), p. 110.

Nuala O'Faolain, 'Real Life in Barrytown', in *Irish Times* (7 November 1992).

Lauren Onkey, 'Celtic Soul Brothers', in *Eire-Ireland*, Vol. 28, part 3 (Fall 1993), pp. 147–58.

Fintan O'Toole, 'Working-Class Dublin on Screen: The Roddy Doyle Films', *Cinéaste*, Vol. 24, nos 2–3 (1999), pp. 36–9.

Ulrike Paschel, *No Mean City? The Image of Dublin in the Novels of Dermot Bolger, Roddy Doyle and Val Mulkerns*, Aachen, British and American Studies, Vol. 10 (Peter Lang, Frankfurt am Main and New York, 1998).

Lorraine Piroux, '"I'm Black an' I'm Proud"': Re-inventing Irishness in Roddy Doyle's *The Commitments*', in *College Literature*, Vol. 25, no. 2 (Spring 1998), pp. 45–58. Reassesses the politics of Doyle's novels.

Colm Tóibín, 'Dublin's Epiphany', *The New Yorker* (3 April 1995), pp. 45–53.

Colm Tóibín, 'New Ways to Kill Your Father', in the *New York Review of Books*, Vol. 50, no. 10 (12 June 2003). A perceptive and carefully worked-out approach to the varying methods and themes in Doyle's work up to *Rory and Ita*. Especially good on Doyle's celebration of the ordinary, as well as discerning on the many genres that he exploits with assurance.

Caramine White, *Reading Roddy Doyle* (Syracuse University Press, New York, 2001). An intelligent and comprehensive assessment up to and including *The Woman Who Walked Into Doors*. An appendix on *A Star Called Henry* brings the work up to date. Also includes a useful interview with the author.

Chrissie Wright, *Paddy Clarke Ha Ha Ha*, in the York Notes series (Longman, London, 1999).

The editors

Jonathan Noakes has taught English in secondary schools in Britain and Australia since 1987. For six years he ran A-level English studies at Eton College where he is a housemaster.

Margaret Reynolds is Reader in English at Queen Mary, University of London, and the presenter of BBC Radio 4's *Adventures in Poetry*. Her publications include *The Sappho Companion* and (with Angela Leighton) *Victorian Women Poets*. Her most recent book is *The Sappho History*.

Vanessa Berman completed her M.A. at the University of London.

ALSO AVAILABLE IN VINTAGE LIVING TEXTS

❑	*American Fiction*	0099445069	£5.99
❑	*Martin Amis*	0099437651	£6.99
❑	*Margaret Atwood*	009943704X	£6.99
❑	*Louis de Bernières*	0099437570	£6.99
❑	*A. S. Byatt*	0099452219	£5.99
❑	*Sebastian Faulks*	0099437562	£6.99
❑	*John Fowles*	0099460882	£5.99
❑	*Ian McEwan*	0099437554	£6.99
❑	*Toni Morrison*	009943766X	£6.99
❑	*Iris Murdoch*	0099452227	£5.99
❑	*Salman Rushdie*	0099437643	£6.99
❑	*Susan Hill*	0099452189	£5.99
❑	*Jeanette Winterson*	0099437678	£6.99

- All Vintage books are available through mail order or from your local bookshop.
- Payment may be made using Access, Visa, Mastercard, Diners Club, Switch and Amex, or cheque, eurocheque and postal order (sterling only).

❑❑❑❑❑❑❑❑❑❑❑❑❑❑❑❑

Expiry Date:＿＿＿＿＿＿＿＿ Signature:＿＿＿＿＿＿＿＿＿＿＿＿＿＿＿

Please allow £2.50 for post and packing for the first book and £1.00 per book thereafter.

ALL ORDERS TO:
Vintage Books, Books by Post, TBS Limited, The Book Service,
Colchester Road, Frating Green, Colchester, Essex, CO7 7DW, UK.
Telephone:　(01206) 256 000
Fax:　　　　(01206) 255 914

NAME: ＿＿＿＿＿＿＿＿＿＿＿＿＿＿＿＿＿＿＿＿＿＿＿＿＿＿＿＿＿＿＿＿

ADDRESS: ＿＿＿＿＿＿＿＿＿＿＿＿＿＿＿＿＿＿＿＿＿＿＿＿＿＿＿＿＿＿

＿＿＿＿＿＿＿＿＿＿＿＿＿＿＿＿＿＿＿＿＿＿＿＿＿＿＿＿＿＿＿＿＿＿＿

＿＿＿＿＿＿＿＿＿＿＿＿＿＿＿＿＿＿＿＿＿＿＿＿＿＿＿＿＿＿＿＿＿＿＿

Please allow 28 days for delivery. Please tick box if you do not wish to
receive any additional information.　　　　　　　　　　　　　　　　❑
Prices and availability subject to change without notice.